25 YI
DUNSTABLE

1952–1977

Commemorating the
Silver Jubilee of HM Queen Elizabeth II

A collection of 400 photographs by

BRUCE TURVEY

The Book Castle

DEDICATION

I dedicate this book to my mother Mrs L. K. Turvey, as my way of saying 'Thank you!' for everything she has done for me.

Contents

First published June 1977 by the author
Republished June 2002 by
The Book Castle
12 Church Street
Dunstable LU5 4RU

ISBN 1 903747 26 0

Printed and bound by Interprint Ltd., Malta
Cover photograph: Queensway Hall and market

Introduction

In July 1975, I put on an exhibition of photographs which I had taken during the twenty-five years I had been in business as a professional photographer in the town.

This exhibition was held in the Dunstable Library and proved so successful (being seen by well over 10,000 people) that I conceived the idea of publishing a book of Dunstable covering just a quarter of a century.

However, this idea was shelved until Christmas 1976, when I realised that 1977 was to be the Queen's Jubilee (1952–77) and I decided to commemorate the occasion by putting on permanent record the same important twenty-five years in the history of Dunstable.

And so in January of this year I took on the mammoth job of selecting and deciding which and how many of the 100,000 photographs which I had taken during these years to use in this book.

I started by looking through twenty-five foolscap diaries, record books and many thousands of negatives, and selecting from around 7,000 assignments suitable material which would be representative of Dunstable during the years 1952–77. These were finally narrowed down to over 800 negatives which were then enlarged and printed, and from these prints 400 were selected and suitably captioned. You can now see the final selection in this book, which puts on permanent record twenty-five years in the history of Dunstable, which I feel were the most important years of the town (at least the most important years of this century).

I have only used photographs which I have taken, I kept all my negatives (except in the case of broken plates) and records and had them permanently filed. Therefore I did not have to rely on other people's photographs.

It was quite impossible for me to record on film every event and every building that has now been demolished during those twenty-five years and some of you may feel that certain photographs should have appeared in this book whether I had taken them myself or not. But even if I had obtained material from elsewhere, there would still have been certain events which would not have been included, so I hope you will understand why certain photographs do not appear.

I have also written all the captions to the photographs and the Diary of Dunstable. It has taken many hundreds of hours in research and checking facts and figures and if there are any inaccuracies then I trust you will bear with me as I have spent only three months in preparing this book for it to be published in time for the Queen's Jubilee.

I have lived in Dunstable for over forty years and to me it is a wonderful town but I do feel that it has lost a lot of its old character as a typical market town. But progress is progress I suppose.

The town, situated on the Watling Street, has become an industrial modern town and I gather from information given to me that it would have cost more to have maintained certain buildings than to demolish and rebuild.

We now have help-yourself stores, help-yourself petrol pumps, double yellow lines which if you park on them can cost you a £6 fine, but all car parking in the town is free.

Large housing estates have now taken the place of many green fields and open spaces that once surrounded the town.

I have enjoyed recording the changing face of Dunstable and the many events that have taken place. To many Dunstablians this book will no doubt bring back some happy and not so happy memories. To the younger and future citizens of Dunstable, may this book serve as a constant reminder that the town of Dunstable during the years 1952–77 did not stand still.

I sincerely hope that you will find this book interesting. If you do then all the work that has been involved in the preparation will have made it all worthwhile.

The book starts with a written diary of Dunstable followed by 400 photographs, in sequence.

The diary covers some events and happenings that do not appear in photographic form, as I did not cover those events or I considered the photographs chosen more interesting or of more importance.

The first photograph shown is of a snow scene and Dunstable received plenty of it in the 1962–63 winter. The last photograph (the 400th) shows a scene during the 1976 heat wave and the shortage of water that we suffered in the long summer of that year.

The other 398 photographs show old buildings that have now been demolished and buildings such as the Town Hall, the *Rifle Volunteer*, and old cottages being demolished.

The Red Lion Hotel, the *White Horse*, the *White Hart*, the *Foresters*, the *Royal Oak*, and the *Queen's Head*, have all disappeared. Shops and businesses that have either been demolished or changed hands include the Criterion Café, Whipsiderry Café, the Dunstable Commercial Hotel, Gibbards Corn Merchants, the Ace Café, Bert England's Motor Cycle Shop, Enterprise Printing Works, the Tuck Shop, Bata Shoes, Andersons Outfitters.

New photographs have been taken from similar viewpoints to show where all the old buildings were and what has now taken their place.

Of all the new developments that have taken place surely the Civic Hall (now Queensway) must rate as one of the most important, with its fantastic acoustics and large hall. So much has been staged in this magnificent hall; banquets, dinners, dances, wrestling contests, exhibitions, shows, keep fit displays and a host of other things, none of which could have taken place in the old Town Hall. To me the Queensway Hall rates as one of the best venues for miles around. A few weeks before it was opened, the new Catholic church in West Street was opened and it was thought to be the first circular church to be built in England for 400 years.

You will see what the California swimming pool used to look like years ago. This pool was classed as the finest swimming pool in Bedfordshire and not only did thousands from all over the county flock there but from other counties as well. (I remember those days so well and I hope some day it may open again.)

You will also see old football teams, cricket teams, darts teams, domino teams, and rugby teams. Coach outings of the past, dinners, dances, parties, New Year's Eve celebrations, retirement photographs, Scout groups and Guide groups.

I have included photographs of the four Prime Ministers who visited the town, and a host of other personalities, including Kenneth More, Sam Kydd, Bob Monkhouse, Arthur Askey, Yolande Pompey, Wilfred Pickles, Brenda Lee, Kathy Kirby, David Kossoff, Kent Walton, The Barron Knights, Reginald Maudling, Hugh Gaitskell and HRH The Duchess of Gloucester (when she opened the Pageant), and Prince William of Gloucester.

There are so many things that I could tell you about the photographs and Dunstable over the last twenty-five years. The memories, the heartaches, the stories that could be told about certain characters that used to be in the town and some that still are. Characters such as 'Coal face' or 'Black face' Charlie, 'Andy' Anderson, Fred White (these are only a few of the names that come to mind), and many more. Another 200 pages could be written. As this is not possible at least for for time being, I will let the readers try to imagine what Dunstable used to be like during the years 1952–1977.

Dunstable Diary – 1952–77

Before beginning the 'Diary' shall we look through some of the prices of everyday items as they were in 1952? These are itemized in decimal figures, so make your own comparisons!

Letter post (only one class)	1p
Printed paper rate	0·6p
Post cards	0·8p
Mild beer – per pint	6p
Bitter beer – per pint	7½p

The *Halfway House* advertised a Christmas offer as follows:

Martell '3 Star' Brandy	£2·20
Whitbread Pale Ale – per dozen	90p
Gordon's Gin	£1·69
Mackesons – per dozen pints	£1·20
20 Player's cigarettes	17½p
1lb best steak	16p
Joint of topside or silverside per lb	15p
Leg of pork per lb	16p

Perhaps you wanted somewhere to live then, the Dunstable Borough *Gazette* was advertising:

Near Dunstable, *three* freehold cottages (one with vacant possession) all containing four rooms, main services – £450 or near offer.

Modern detached bungalow containing three bedrooms, two reception rooms, tiled bathroom, domestic office, detached garage with one acre of land – £3,000.

A plot of land in Kingsway with 60ft frontage, freehold offered by Connell's estate agents for £250.

Cotton blankets at £2·00 per pair and a piano at £40·95.

You have your house, so what about some entertainment?

A washing machine from Arthur Chattell at £40 or rent a television set at 12½p per week? Or perhaps ringside seat at the wrestling at 40p (12½p standing) or dancing classes at the *White Hart* for 7½p?

Now how about a holiday? A day at the gymkhana cost 5p, an inclusive holiday in Britain was advertised at only £10·15 per week, holiday camps £5·25 weekly from Travel House or Continental holidays for £15·10. A Bournemouth hotel with h & c, central heating, radio in each room and free car parking was a bit expensive at £7·35 for a week.

Owing to the shortage of new cars, however, ownership was relatively expensive. One had to be in quite a high income bracket to afford a P4 Rover 75, two years old, offered by Camden Motors at £2,095. A fourteen year old Ford 10 would fetch around £300.

Fifteen to 16-year-old shop assistants were required at £2 to £2·25 per week and, surprise, J. W. Green Ltd (now Whitbreads) were announcing that they may have to increase their beer prices.

1952

JANUARY On the sports front *First & Last* (both male and female teams) lead in the LV Darts League and Waterlows were leading in the Works League. The *Sugar Loaf* Tap were leading the Dunstable League.

Dunstable Town Football Club were in the Metropolitan & South Midland League under the chairmanship of Councillor J. J. Gracy and lost 1–6 to Luton Town 'A' in the second round of the Metropolitan Cup.

The *Bull* lead in Dunstable Domino League.

Former chairman of Dunstable Liberal Club and secretary of Waterlow's Sports Association for man years Mr William Markham died aged 70.

Few vacancies for jobs in the town.

FEBRUARY On the 8th, Alderman Tom Sandland read to the townspeople the Accession of Queen Elizabeth II to the throne following the death of her father King George VI on the 6th of the month.

Mr Norman Cole became Tory member of Parliament for South Beds.

There was an increase of 4p to 9p per week in Council house rents.

MARCH Beecroft Primary School opens.

Owing to a steel shortage 140 A.C. Sphinx workers went on a four-day week and a further sixty-seven were laid off.

Dunstable rate drops 1p to 62½p in the £.

MAY Headmistress of Burr Street School Miss Boyes retires after twenty-six years.

Dunstable Building Society shares were available for 50p per month, with 2½ per cent interest per annum.

Whipsnade Zoo celebrated its 21st birthday.

Three Dunstable Councillors were defeated in municipal elections – Cllr Mrs D. M. Mills, Cllr J. H. Hillman, and Cllr H. W. M. Richards.

First & Last won the Ladies' Darts League.

A champion steer was sold at Dunstable cattle market for £116·50, it weighed 16 cwt. He was the champion of Thame Agricultural Show.

War memorial unveiled in Priory Meadow on 9 May.

JUNE Experienced groundsman was required by Northfields School. He had to have knowledge of machinery and ability to drive was essential; and for this they were willing to pay £6·26 per week (imagine buying one of those cars on this sort of money).

Coronation was proclaimed by the Mayor Ald B. J. Scott, and from the Town Hall steps announced the date as 2 June 1953.

The *Sugar Loaf* Tap won the League Championship, the Whitbread Cup and the individual and foursomes competitions in the Dunstable & District Darts League.

National Savings in Dunstable totalled £6,822 for one week.

There was a mile long procession in the fourth annual carnival and fête.

JULY BBC radio programme *Down Your Way* team visited Dunstable with Richard Dimbleby, and the Council were not too happy about the way the programme was produced.

AUGUST An 80ft well discovered fifty yards from Town Hall when a workman narrowly escaped death when ground gave way.

Famous golfers visited Dunstable Downs Golf Club for qualifying round of the *News of the World* Professional Championship. Among them were Henry Cotton, Dai Rees, Tom Haliburton, Ken Bousfield, Max Faulkner and Flory Van Dorck.

SEPTEMBER Forty young Dunstable men registered for National Service.
Road islands completed in the High Street.
NOVEMBER 700 Dunstable people on housing list.
1st – A.C. Sphinx Spark Plug Co changed their name to A.C. Delco Division of General Motors Ltd (A.C. Delco moved to Dunstable in 1934).
Seventy private building licences were sanctioned by Dunstable Town Council.
Dunstable welcomed the abolishment of land development charge. Builders believe this will lead to increased private building.
30th – The Prime Minister of Pakistan Mr Khwaja Nazimuddin an old boy of Dunstable Grammar Schoo revisited his old school after forty years.
DECEMBER 500th postwar dwelling house completed on Beecroft Estate.

1953 (the year of the Coronation)
MARCH Big decrease in number of accidents at A.C. Delco.
Local preacher in the Methodist Connexion J. H. Hillman of Dunstable completes fifty years.
Dunstable becomes highest rated borough in the county at £1·40 in £.
APRIL Memorial service held in the Priory for the late Queen Mary who died at the end of March.
Chief Inspector H. G. Woods takes over as new Police Supt at Dunstable from Supt T. E. S. Turton.
Average earnings of a Dunstable Vauxhall worker was just over £10 per week.
Only forty-eight people *unemployed* in the whole of Dunstable – thirty-two men and sixteen women.
JUNE 2nd – Dunstable celebrated Coronation day in grand fashion with carnival procession, fireworks display, dancing, beer barrel rolling, torchlight procession, children's street parties, etc etc, in very cold and bleak weather.
JULY Work starts on new Commer Cars factory in Boscombe Road (opposite Vauxhall Motors). Estimated cost £1 million.
AUGUST Dunstable Girls' Choir appeared on television on *Carol Levis and his Discoveries* Show.
SEPTEMBER Thomas Tilling Ltd purchase controlling interest in Bagshawe's.
OCTOBER Dunstable magistrates believe that 11.00 pm for extensions is quite enough for functions (how times have changed: pubs used to close at 10.00 pm in those days).
NOVEMBER Clarkes of Dunstable were offering a 25-piece dinner service for 95p.
Council agree to spend £3,013 on building pair of houses at Downside and these are the dearer ones, the cheaper ones costing £2,848 per pair.
DECEMBER Two Dunstable men were each fined a total of £20 for passing betting slips in the *Plume of Feathers* and *Nag's Head* (no betting shops in those days).

1954
JANUARY Sir Edgar Waterlow, chairman of Waterlow & Sons dies at the age of 83.
FEBRUARY Bell from the cemetery chapel was sold for £22.
Large loaf from Lyons cost 3½p, February 1977 price on average is 23p.
Five bus shelters erected in town at a cost of £336.
MARCH Estimated expenditure on repairs and maintenance for town's housing estates for year ending March 1955 was £14,071.
Chade Razor Blade Co at High Street South closes down and alternative employment is offered to the eighty employees.
A reduction in the rates of 8½p in £.
APRIL Dunstable Young People's Club opens (using the premises of the Pioneer Boys' Club).
MAY Former Labour Chancellor of the Exchequer (the late) Rt Hon Hugh Gaitskell visits Dunstable, but only a small audience turned up at the Town Hall to hear him.
JUNE Between 250–300 houses in the town were unfit for habitation, this was stated by Mr A. Bishop the town's Senior Sanitary Inspector.
JULY There was no rush to local butchers following the de-rationing of meat.
Dunstable Town Council paid £20 funeral expenses of a local person who died (as under Section 50 of the National Assistance Act of 1948 they were apparently responsible for these expenses).
AUGUST Only twenty-three people out of work in the area – fourteen men and nine women.
Demands for labour on the increase.
SEPTEMBER 1st – Hadrian Estate opened by (the late) Ald W. H. Robinson, Mayor.
OCTOBER £1 million order for Commer diesel engine from British buyers.
Canon Orton becomes Rector of Dunstable Priory.
DECEMBER 71,300 letters received at Dunstable Post Office in a single day – 14 per cent up on previous year.
31st – Mr H. W. Small, president of Dunstable & District Chamber of Trade, gives us this quote on which to end 1954 – 'When history comes to be written it will prove that 1954 will go down as the most memorable year of the century' (only time will tell! Author).

1955
JANUARY The town has the best housing record in Bedfordshire.
H. H. Todd becomes works general manager of Waterlow & Sons and his son Roland becomes works manager.
FEBRUARY Work of lowering the road beneath the railway bridge at High Street North starts at £1,000 per inch. The road was lowered 14½ inches.
P. N. Wainwright becomes sub-manager of Midland Bank.
F. G. Wilks retired as manager of Barclays Bank.
Vauxhall workers get 0·6p to 1·6p per hour rise (hourly paid workers).
APRIL Council house rents go up 4p per week.
Good Friday orange rolling at the Downs revived.
Bernard Hunt, Peter Allis, Dai Rees play at Dunstable Downs Golf Club for Stewart Field (club professional) Benefit Match.
MAY Labour have setbacks at municipal elections.
Dunstable celebrates tenth anniversary of VE Day.
JUNE Skeleton of Saxon warrior about AD 450 found on Puddle Hill.
Tornado hits Dunstable but no damage was sustained, it didn't touch the ground.
AUGUST 3rd – The cattle market on the Square closed down. Moved to Tavistock Street for a short period.
SEPTEMBER Erection of 168ft high pylons for the 275,000 volt national grid begins over Blows Downs. There was a lot of controversy over this as to why it should come through Dunstable.
300 chairs were destroyed by fire at the municipal offices. Flames reached 30ft high.
NOVEMBER Cross Paperware factory practically gutted by fire but work carried on.

1956
FEBRUARY Dunstable was one of the coldest places in the country with 25 degrees of frost.

Ald T. Sandland takes over as chairman of Dunstable Town Football Club following the resignation of J. J. Gracy.

Police Supt H. Woods reported a startling rise in drunkeness in the town.

MARCH Rates down to 86p in the £, but most people had to pay more because of increased assessments.

APRIL Large traffic hold ups in the town over the Easter weekend.

MAY Duke of Edinburgh opens new Ludun factory at Liscombe Road.

JULY Meteorological weather forecasting station moves to Bracknell in Berkshire after being at Drovers Way, Dunstable during the second world war. Several attempts were made to bomb the station and the German planes used to drop silver strips of paper over the pylons to upset the radio waves. One German bomb was actually dropped opposite the station in Totternhoe Road between two bungalows, but to the relief of all the residents (including myself) remained unexploded.

AUGUST Well known antique dealer Harry Rixon dies aged 78.

August Bank Holiday was very wet.

More and more in Dunstable turn to television – two televisions to every three homes in the Dunstable area. The television licence in those days was £3.

OCTOBER Seventy electricians employed by sub-contractors go out on strike at Vauxhall Motors.

NOVEMBER The Mayor Ald W. T. Lack buys the first Premium Bond to be issued in Dunstable.

There were large queues at the post office for petrol coupons and the local industries were hit by the petrol crisis.

DECEMBER Bottle of Gordon's Gin was £1·69 in 1952 was advertised in 1956 for £1·70, going up 1p in four years (hard to believe, well they really were the good old days).

There were 991 houses and flats occupied on Beecroft, Brewers Hill and Dunstable Estates. On the housing list 188 were on the live list and 179 on the deferred list.

30th – Mr and Mrs P. Vickers moved into the 1,000th postwar house to be built in Dunstable and this was the achievement for the year of 1956.

1957
MARCH Dunstable & District Chamber of Trade were concerned by loss of business due to inadequate parking facilities.

JULY Houses on Downside Estate were being pestered by earwigs, they were found in people's clothes, their beds, in food and in fact everywhere. This was mainly at the south end of the estate near the rubber company.

A sixth century Saxon burial ground was unearthed at Marina Drive by Manshead Archaeological Society of Dunstable.

SEPTEMBER 15th – Father Evelco Ortiz bids farewell to the Catholic church after being priest in charge for twelve and a half years.

OCTOBER Downside Estate rents varied between £2·50–£3 per week and there were 349 names on the housing list.

NOVEMBER 70 mph gusts recorded in the town causing severe damage including nearly 200 television aerials and masts blown down.

DECEMBER Bottle of gin went up by 4p during year to £1·74 per bottle.

Chickens were selling 25p per lb, turkeys 22½p to 30p per lb – prices for these in February 1977 had only risen a few pence in twenty years. Chickens were selling on average about 35p per lb and turkeys about 43p per lb.

Bottle of '5 star' French brandy would have cost you £1·80.

1958
JANUARY The year started off on a sad note when forty-one piglets died in a fire at Manor Farm, Sewell.

Vauxhall Motors present the Mayor of Dunstable with the *Mayoral* car.

Council rents go up yet again, this time with a rise of between 7½p and 10p per week – about a 4 per cent increase.

FEBRUARY The worst snow blizzard for eleven years hits Dunstable.

APRIL Only a 25 per cent poll at local elections.

MAY Ald W. T. Lack becomes Mayor for third year running.

Revd Christopher MacKonochie becomes new Rector of Priory Church.

JUNE Dunstable Grammar School started in 1888 now seventy years old. Six of the school boys went to Buckingham Palace to collect gold awards from the Duke of Edinburgh Prince Philip.

Hedley Manwaring well known local hotelier and town councillor for sixteen years (1934–50) died.

A 2,000 year old bread roll found at Puddle Hill.

Rt Hon Henry Brooke the then Minister of Housing and Local Government opens the new £314,000 sewage works at Chalk Hill.

JULY The new *Eight Bells* opens in Westfield Road after the old *Eight Bells* had been demolished in Ashton Street.

AUGUST Demolition of the top end of Church Street started for the road widening scheme.

OCTOBER 29 acres of building land at Poynters Road and Hadrian Avenue were sold for £71,500, and 300 bungalows and houses were planned for the site.

Dunstable Town Council had a few unfurnished maisonettes to let at £3·67½ per week exclusive of rates.

1959
This was the year that the whole Civic Centre plan including the now (renamed) Queensway Hall, Recreation Centre, the Library, College, Ambulance Station, Court House, Market, Shopping Precinct, car parks *was conceived* by a group of gentlemen standing on the railway bridge in Dog Kennel Lane (that is a lane dividing High Street North by the Grove House Gardens with Houghton Regis). Among these gents were Jack Smith (the Town Clerk at that time), George Brewis (Clerk to the County Council), the late Ron Carrington (the Town Borough Surveyor at that time) and Michael L. Kilby (who represented Dunstable Borough Council), they looked towards the Town Hall clock and between them and the clock lay some 24 acres of unused land. They all agreed that they should aim to purchase the land that had some old army Nissen huts (left over from the war) and some unkept allotments. The idea was to accommodate a new Civic hall and Civic buildings together with the new Quadrant shopping centre and car parks, so that everything adjoined each other and with easy access, and also to open up and blend the Grove House Gardens into the overall new development. Mr Brewis and Mr Smith were a little worried, however, as they believed the public would not go along with such a scheme as it was looking too far ahead. However, the overall plan was submitted to the various committees of their respective Councils and was approved in 1960. Land was purchased and buildings were commenced in 1961 and I for one am pleased that those four gents met on Dog Kennel Bridge one Saturday morning in 1959.

Also this year saw the start of the Winkle Club at the *Star & Garter*. This was started by Mr Alec Horsler (the then landlord of the pub). Members of this club pay just a small initial subscription and they are then given a 'winkle' shell and a small fine is imposed on them if they are caught without their 'winkle'. The main purpose of this club is to raise money for the local firm 'Ludun' which employs disabled people on a non profit basis. In the first year of the club, £94 was raised and at February 1977 this had reached a staggering figure of over £11,500.

JANUARY *Have a Go* the radio programme with Wilfred Pickles and Mabel (his wife) visited Dunstable and the show was broadcast live from the Town Hall.

The town experienced the most difficult winter conditions for twelve years (1947) and there were over fifty accidents along the Watling Street.

Dunstable Excelsior Band appeared on BBC *Tonight* programme with personality Derek Hart.

Well known George Cox local gents outfitter of Flinte House and former town councillor died.

FEBRUARY Rent for some council houses in Garden Road was £1·30 per week.

MARCH The 10 acre site of the Meadway Hostel together with the chalets were auctioned for £34,000.

There was another decrease in the rates.

APRIL A former local estate agent was sent to prison for two and a half years for wholesale 'Filching' of clients' money. He was said to have had a sort of 'Jekyl and Hyde' personality, and was spending at the rate of £100 per week. (The equivalent of this today would be about £400 to £500 per week.)

The death-watch beetle hit the Priory Church again.

MAY A tender of £37,422 was accepted by the Council to build twenty-three old people's dwellings at Downside.

SEPTEMBER Queen Eleanor's School for girls opens in Langdale Road (the new headmistress was Miss Christina Scott, a Dunstable person).

St Augustine's Church at Downside opened.

OCTOBER Harold William Parrott has the Freedom of the Borough conferred on him.

Rt Hon Harold Macmillan (Prime Minister 1957–63) visits the town.

Dunstable Town Football Club issued 20,000 shares at 25p each.

NOVEMBER On the 21st of this month the M1 was opened (the first motorway in the country) and the traffic through Dunstable was decreased by 50 per cent.

DECEMBER On the 10th of this month the *Highwayman* Motel was opened in London Road.

Waterlow's showed a loss of £296,933.

Christmas turkeys were selling at the same price as two years previous 1957 22½p–30p per lb.

The 50,000th Bedford truck came off the line at Dunstable Vauxhall.

Before we leave the 1950s a mention must be given to Brian Martin an outstanding local cricketer who played for Dunstable Town, APCM and the county and who scored century after century.

1960

JANUARY Ald W. T. Lack Deputy Mayor and former Mayor of Dunstable and also second master at Dunstable Grammar School was awarded the OBE for political and public services.

33,200 cigarettes were stolen from Hayhoe's newsagents and tobacconists in High Street South.

There were 9 degrees of frost, icy winds, slippery roads; and 25 tons of grit were put down due to this.

A Dunstable man was jailed for driving a 3-inch nail into his pet dog, a bull mastiff; a dog he loved.

The Council purchase the land known as Park Estate for the proposed new Civic buildings, etc (as mentioned in the 1959 diary) 22·06 acres for the sum of £137,876.

WVS take over and run the 'Meals on Wheels' service.

MARCH A former Dunstable Alderman Reginald Eric Gibbons dies aged 57.

Purnell & Sons of Bristol make a bid worth £2·15 million for Waterlow's.

2nd – The California Ballroom opens.

Well known butcher Harold White dies aged 43.

APRIL Mrs Beavington becomes new president of Dunstable & District Chamber of Trade.

New pavilion opens at Bennetts Recreation Ground.

AUGUST 26th – Scotland Yard called in to investigate the death of a man whose body was found under a slag heap on part of Dunstable Downs.

Mr E. W. Green offered to sell the California pool, the ballroom, restaurant, skating rink and sports stadium to Dunstable Borough Council. No figure was mentioned (at least no record found to this effect).

NOVEMBER 200 workers put on three-day week at A.C. Delco.

Cross Paperware gutted by fire again (second big fire in five years).

DECEMBER On the 8th of this month the telephone exchange goes automatic.

1961

JANUARY Dunstable man, a 30 year old car salesman, was charged with murder (see August 1960). He was found guilty at Beds Assizes on the 20th of this month and sentenced to death. Several appeals and a petition were made against the sentence, but all to no avail and he was hanged at Bedford Jail on 29 March 1961. It was the first hanging in Bedford prison for more than twenty years and was also one of the last in this country before the abolition of the death penalty.

FEBRUARY Lieut-Col Sir Deltry Charles Part, OBE a well-known local figure of Houghton Hall died at the age of 78.

The death was also reported of well known local solicitor Norman Gutteridge aged 73.

MARCH Employees share out of profit at A.C. Delco equivalent to one and a half weeks' wages.

Rates go up to 111 new pence in the £ an increase of just over ½p over 1960.

APRIL A Dunstable couple, Mr Maurice Stone and his wife Ann, together with four other men set out from the town on a 70,000 mile expedition through Europe, Jerusalem, Turkey, Burma, Australia, New Zealand, Vancouver and America. They set off in two Land-Rovers.

JUNE The 1961 census showed that the population of Dunstable was 25,618.

The unemployed in Dunstable totalled sixty-five but there were 202 vacancies for jobs.

JULY The Church Street road widening starts.

SEPTEMBER Some Commer men go on four-day week and then later 460 were laid off.

OCTOBER Dunstable Borough *Gazette* went up in price by 1p to 1½p, the first increase in ten years. (How's that compared with the inflation we have nowadays.)

NOVEMBER H. H. Todd former managing director of Waterlows died at the age of 65.

DECEMBER Commers were back to full production plus overtime.

Revd R. French former Rector of the Priory Church died aged 78.

1962

JANUARY The year started with weather conditions of snow, ice, fog, wind and very, very cold.

Old Palace Lodge was granted a full licence.

Hundreds of Dunstablians rush to the clinic to have smallpox vaccinations, following outbreak of smallpox in Britain.

FEBRUARY Yet again Police Supt Horace Woods reported a rise in drunkeness in the town.
MARCH Estimated cost of the new Civic centre was given as £311,643.
Foundation stone was laid for the new Catholic church.
On 2 March a tragic accident took place in Poynters Road in which three long-standing Waterlow's employees were killed in a head-on crash after they had attended their firm's annual Ex-Service Men's Association dinner at the *Halfway House*. They were Mr George Wilkins, Mr Ernest Charles Taylor and Mr Leslie Howlett – all were respected and it was indeed a very tragic loss which everyone who attended that dinner (including myself) will never forget.
MAY Labour win three seats from Conservatives in municipal elections.
JULY For all those leaving school there were sufficient jobs in the town.
SEPTEMBER On the 17th of this month the new Young People's Club opened and on 1 November the new Pioneer Boys' Club opened. The clubs are next to one another in Manchester Place.
DECEMBER The new railway bridge in Church Street was completed.

1963
JANUARY This year started off with one of the worst cold spells ever to hit Dunstable, the Zoo was completely cut off from the outside world and the steward of the Dunstable Downs Golf Club, his wife and their two children were marooned in the clubhouse.
At the end of January, due to the arctic conditions, there were a lot of power failures. Some homes had no electric lights for eighteen hours due to frozen cables.
MARCH On the 4th of this month the *White Horse*, Church Street closed down.
There was still a lot of snow about, especially on the Downs.
The *Red Lion*, High Street North closed down on the 15th of this month.
The Dunstable rate was the lowest in the county.
APRIL Headmaster of Northfields School Mr F. Langley retires.
Police Inspector John left the town to go to Luton. He had been with the Dunstable Police for sixteen years.
MAY Ald M. L. Kilby aged 38 becomes the youngest Mayor the town has ever had. He took over from Cllr Haydn W. Parrott.
JUNE On 4 June Dunstable saw the pageant performed in the Priory Meadow. Over 1,000 local performers took part in which 800 years of Dunstable was depicted. The pageant was opened by HRH The Duchess of Gloucester.
JULY On the 8th of this month Dunstable's new Post Office opened in High Street North at a cost of £79,400.
Headmaster at Priory School (formerly Britain Street School) Mr J. G. Watson retired after seventeen years. He had in fact been headmaster in Bedfordshire for thirty-two years.
Another local headmaster Mr L. H. Cunningham head of Ashton Primary School retired after nineteen years.
The new court house was opened.
SEPTEMBER A 32-year-old Lithuanian woman Eleanor Vistartus was found battered to death in her home. Later a man admitted killing her and was sent for trial and jailed for seven years after the jury brought in the verdict of manslaughter.
OCTOBER On 20 October Priory Church service was televised on ATV.
NOVEMBER On 21 November Eliza Neal of High Street South celebrated her 100th birthday.
DECEMBER 500th house was built on Croft Estate.

1964 (DUNSTABLE'S CENTENARY YEAR)
It was 100 years previous that Dunstable had its own Borough Council, the Charter incorporation took place on 8 December 1864.
JANUARY The 'Rolling Stones' (the then No 1 pop group) performed at the California Ballroom.
Workers' Playtime was broadcast live from Commer Cars.
FEBRUARY The Council have an extra expense of £3,000 for resiting of a bar in the Civic hall, this upset the ratepayers.
MARCH On 15 March the Catholic church was opened at West Street in a snowstorm.
The market stalls in High Street North close down after many years and now move to the new site at Queensway car park.
APRIL On 16 April the new Civic hall was opened (later renamed Queensway) by the Lord Mayor of London Sir James Harman at a cost of around £320,000. The catering and bars were in the hands of Mr Peter Aiken who also raises many thousands of pounds for LV Homes. It was understood that Mr Aiken would be leaving the Queensway Hall later this year (1977) after thirteen years.
MAY Labour members of Council walk out of a special purposes committee after a full scale row developed.
Seamus Dunne former Luton Town player takes over as player-manager for Dunstable Town FC.
JUNE 3rd East Anglian Regiment receive the Freedom of the Borough.
OCTOBER On 7 October Sir Alec Douglas-Home (the then Prime Minister) visited the Square, Dunstable to deliver his election speech to thousands of local people who literally packed the Square.
On 16 October the Conservatives held South Beds with Norman Cole winning by only 339 votes from P. J. Nisbett (Labour) in the 1964 General Election.

1965
JANUARY To start the year yet again there were more blizzards and snowdrifts with buses and cars getting stuck.
Mr and Mrs Maurice Stone return after their almost 80,000 mile trip around the world, this included spending a year in Australia *working aboard a 6,000 ton liner as stewards*.
Well known Mr Melville Scott Lockhart died aged 83.
FEBRUARY Dunstable hold memorial service in the Civic Hall for Sir Winston Churchill who died on 24 January.
APRIL Passenger services to Dunstable railway station end. The last train 'The Skimpot Flyer' left Dunstable North station at 7.25 pm on 24 April for Welwyn, Herts (the first train to enter Dunstable was on 3 May, 1858 when the line opened).
An Electrolux fridge was selling for £38·85 for 3·4 cu.ft model.
Well-known Mr Peter Allen a former Councillor and Alderman and proprietor of the *Sugar Loaf* Hotel died suddenly. It came as a shock to all who knew him.

MAY 800 Dunstablians attended a public meeting at the Queensway Hall to discuss proposals for a Dunstable ring road. Many meetings were held to discuss this project and many aspects were looked at including costs, inconvenience, compensation, etc. A committee of the Dunstable Ring Road Resistance Association was formed (its chairman was Peter Delaporte) to handle and fight the proposals that the

Beds County Council put forward, and in the end after some hard-fought battles over many years the ring road scheme never went through.

An Austin Princess was purchased by the Council for the Mayor's official use, this would be chauffeur-driven (the Mayor's chauffeur at that time was Mr F. West), the Mayor at that time was Ald L. C. Worby.

Prices of cars were more realistic a one year old Vauxhall Victor was selling for around £565.

JUNE Taximen of Dunstable were incensed that there had been no increase in fares for seventeen years since 1 February 1948 and they were finding great difficulty in making a living and a letter on their behalf was sent to the Council who control taxi fares; but fares remained the same, which were at that time 9p for the first mile and 4p for each subsequent ½ mile or 25p for the first hour and 6p for each subsequent ¼ hour. The Council replied by stating that all taxi fares have to be approved by the Home Office.

A Dunstable postman could have earned £14 per week.

The Dunstable Borough *Gazette* had been going for 100 years.

JULY The Bomb Disposal Squad were called in when a smoke bomb was found on an allotment in Westfield Road.

The *White Hart* in High Street North closed down.

AUGUST On the 9th of this month the *Winston Churchill*, Church Street was opened, at a cost of £35,000 to build.

OCTOBER The new fire station at Brewers Hill Road opened.

NOVEMBER Waterlow Automation Services begin production in a building which then had the largest unsupported span in Europe. Each is 180ft in length and weighs 3 tons. They produce computer and teleprinter tapes.

The Town Hall was sold to the Pearl Assurance Co Ltd for £35,000. It was sold by auction at the *Old Sugar Loaf* by Mr Ken Ball of Connells.

DECEMBER A local club treasurer gassed himself after being short of funds to pay out from the savings club.

A well known local 'Roadster' known as just 'Coal Black' Charlie was accidentally killed in a road accident near Thorn Turn, Chalk Hill, Dunstable. He was aged 80 and was quite a 'loved character'.

1966

JANUARY On the 25th of this month Jack Smith resigned from his office after serving nearly sixteen years as the Borough of Dunstable Town Clerk.

FEBRUARY A greyhound known as 'High Joe' which was kidnapped from kennels in Thornwood, Essex, was found in a garage in Evelyn Road, Dunstable. The greyhound was early favourite for the 1965 Greyhound Derby and was valued at £5,000. A catchphrase that used to be said about the disappearance of the dog was – 'I hear they've found "High Joe"' (one would say to another) and the reply would be 'Where', the first person would reply 'Outside Barking!' (a town in Essex).

MARCH On 24 March the Rt Hon Harold Wilson (now 'Sir' and the then Prime Minister 1964–70 and 1974–76) visits Queensway Hall to deliver election speech. There was a noisy reception from hecklers.

On the 25th of this month the BBC radio programme *Friday Night is Music Night* was broadcast live from the Queensway Hall.

APRIL Gwilym Roberts becomes new Member of Parliament for South Beds after defeating Norman Cole by 4.230 votes. Mr Roberts is now MP for Cannock.

An audience of only fifty greeted the first night of the drama festival at the Queensway Hall.

MAY Conservatives gain control of the Council at the municipal elections.

On 27 May well-known local doctor Dr Blount dies aged 76.

JUNE On the 3rd of this month Bob Monkhouse opened the Quadrant shopping centre. Bob is very well known as a comedian and as the compere of the ITV show *The Golden Shot*, and the more recent television show *Celebrity Squares*.

JULY The Town Hall was demolished.

Cross Paperware ship 661 cartons to Sydney, Australia their biggest ever order (up to then) worth more than £7,000.

AUGUST Permission for a gaming club in 54 High Street South was granted.

OCTOBER On 3 October Cesar's Palace opens with Tommy Cooper (comedian and magician who also had his own show on television). Tommy stayed at the *Sugar Loaf* Hotel during the week he was appearing at Cesars and when he arrived at the *Sugar Loaf* he had forgotten to pack his 'braces', so the manager of the *Sugar Loaf* at that time (Mr Tony Spencer) loaned him some (part of the hotel service).

Dunstable Town Football Club were in financial trouble, Seamus Dunne (the manager) stated they may have to withdraw from the Southern League.

The Revd Charles inducted at the Priory Church to take over as new Rector.

The Youth Club were £842 in debt and in danger of closing stated the leader at that time Alf Hart.

Tesco Stores were raided and £1,000 worth of foodstuffs were stolen.

NOVEMBER Four year old Jacqueline Smith won a car in a Licensed Victuallers draw.

The plans for the gaming club in High Street South falls through, no reason was given for this.

F. J. Creak former Mayor of the town from 1923–24 and a Councillor and Alderman from 1919 to 1931 died at the age of 97, he also appeared on the *Have a Go* radio show in 1959.

1967

JANUARY Dunstable North station demolished following its closure in 1965.

Dunstable Travel Agency advertised a ten-day holiday in Austria from £19·95 (19gns) and you could have had an air-coach holiday for twelve days in the Canary Islands from £42·20 (44 gns).

J. A. C. Bain resigns as chairman of Dunstable Town FC. Clem Stone takes over and stated that there was no likelihood of the club withdrawing from the league.

Cross Paperware lost £2,000 to £3,000 in lost production when half the staff walked out because it was too cold to work.

FEBRUARY Ald Walter Creasey died after a long illness aged 57. He was a former Mayor 1965–66 and had served on the Town Council for twelve years being chairman of many committees. 'Wally' as he was known to the thousands of people had been a licensee for thirty-three years and took over the *Halfway House* in 1939 (twenty-eight years previous). He also acquired the *Glen Eagles* Hotel at Harpenden. There are so many things that could be written about Walter Creasey but unfortunately space does not permit. 'Wally' did so much for this town and the old people that lived in it. He built the *Halfway House* up into one of the best known venues for miles around and to those of you who ever attended a dinner there, you will know what I mean when I say that 'Everything had to be just right'. A personal friend of mine, I can only finish by saying that Dunstable lost a good citizen (and a friend) when Walter Creasey died.

Another former Mayor 1946–49 Albert William Banks aged 86 died one day after Walter Creasey.

The new library opened at a cost of £75,000 and quickly gained 2,000 new members.

MARCH The Dunstable & District Horticultural Society was disbanded when the twice yearly shows were stopped when membership dropped from 300 to only sixty.

There were staff redundancies at A.C. Delco.

APRIL Fire broke out at the new gas board plant. No one was injured and very little damage was done, but the highly inflammable oil and gas tanks were threatened.
JUNE £5,000 was spent on rectifying faults found in the new fire station which had only been open for just under two years.
AUGUST The unveiling of a plaque took place at the football club to commemorate the renaming of Dunstable Town Football Club, Brewers Hill to 'Creasey Park' in memory of the late Ald Walter Creasey. The unveiling ceremony was performed by his wife Joyce.
NOVEMBER The Rt Hon Edward Heath visits Dunstable.
DECEMBER Twenty-eight men walk out from the Experimental Dept at A.C. Delco as they were refused equal status with the rest of the engineering personnel.

Commers work to rule.

Busmen strike – schoolchildren walk to school and many other people either gave lifts or accepted them.

An experiment was tried at the centre crossroads with no right-hand turn into High Street South coming from West Street. All the people who were questioned agreed that this was no answer to the crossroads' problem (and I entirely agree with them. Author). When will something be done?

1968
JANUARY Blizzards start the year yet again and workers were arriving late. One person who could not get on a bus at the Luton and Dunstable Hospital began to walk to his work in Dunstable and so bad were the traffic conditions that he overtook the bus by the *Halfway House* a mile further on.
FEBRUARY On the 15th of this month Dunstable's oldest inhabitant Eliza Neill of 141 High Street South dies aged 104.
MARCH A 'no questions asked' amnesty to hand in any guns to Dunstable Police Station resulted in a machine gun being handed in.

Local traders decide no longer to sponsor the 100 year old custom of 'orange rolling' on Dunstable Downs (at Pascombe Pit).

Beds County Council decide to go ahead with its plan for a hostel for mentally handicapped in Lancot Drive in spite of objections by Dunstable (and at the time of going to press nothing has been done yet).
APRIL Seamus Dunne Dunstable Town manager for four years sacked.
MAY New Polish Church opened in Victoria Street after taking over the Victoria Street Methodist Church.

St Fremund's Church, Westfield Road dedicated by the Bishop of St Albans.
JUNE A mother and her two children were found dead in their Langdale Road home. The husband and father was charged with murdering one of the children a 7-year-old girl. He later pleaded guilty to manslaughter of all three and was jailed for five years. He used potassium cyanide to kill them.

Len Chalmers a former Leicester full-back takes over as manager of Dunstable Town.
SEPTEMBER The payroll of £11,000 for employees of the Empire Rubber Co (now Miles Redfern), London Road was snatched in a daring raid on the firm's car carrying the money. Three masked men used coshes and a fire extinguisher.
OCTOBER Herts and Beds Yeomanry receive the Freedom of the Borough.

The Dunstable Repertory Co have their very own theatre opened by Bernard Bresslaw (well-known actor) after taking over and renovating the old library in High Street South and they named it 'The Little Theatre'.
NOVEMBER The 'Key' Club opened in West Street (but later closed down, see also February 1971).

Our local and the then 'World' beer-drinking champion Lionel Tutt was seen in action on the television programme *The Dave Allen Show*, he sunk seventeen pints of beer in 35 minutes.
DECEMBER The crossroad experiment ended after twelve months (and what the authorities learnt by it I'll never know; just take a look at those crossroads today. Author).

Tom Moore secretary of the Dunstable Downs Golf Club for forty years retired.

1969
JANUARY The year started with New Year's Eve hangovers and a number of employees absent from their work.

Sixty employees from Commers went on unofficial strike.

Once again there was plenty of snow about.

A £1,000 ring was stolen from a jewellers in the Quadrant and bystanders refused to help as the assistan chased the thief.

Local people could not be given a blood test after being breathalised because local police surgeon resigned because of a claim by the BMA for better rates for doing this kind of work.

Bingo begins at the ABC Cinema to a packed house. There was a long queue outside for two hours before the doors opened.

Syntilla Mfg of Luton Road closed down and eighty workers protested about being kept in the dark about this. The firm later moved to Blackpool.

Priory Church service was on London Weekend Television.
FEBRUARY Local boxer Cliff Field started his first two professional fights in spectacular fashion, he spent less than eight minutes in the ring, knocking out his first opponent in just 133 seconds and his second opponent in less than five minutes. He became known as a knockout specialist and his next opponent and many more withdrew from the arranged contests with him. He was just too good and it became difficult to find suitable opponents, but those that were found he just kept beating. In February 1970 he was rated 12th in the British heavyweight title ratings and in April of that year he decided to emigrate to Canada because he thought there would be better opportunities; but because he went without his manager's permission, a ban was put on his boxing in Canada by the Canadian Boxing Board. He returned three months later in July 1970 and was left without a place in the top fifteen ratings of British heavyweights. On 19 October 1971 he sparred two rounds at the Albert Hall with no other than Cassius Clay (Mohammed Ali) ('I'm the greatest') in an exhibition bout. Poor Cliff's short boxing career seemed to be stemmed with so many disappointments which seemed to have started when he was in the Navy, when he had no end of trouble getting out of the Navy to fight. Cliff's boxing career finally came to an end in December 1973, when he was forced to give it up on medical grounds after only 15 professional fights. Who knows Dunstable may well have had a heavyweight champion.

More blizzards and cars get stuck with Whipsnade Road being blocked.

Another rate increase of 15p to 18p in the £.
MARCH The 1½ millionth Bedford truck comes off the Dunstable Vauxhall production line. Anthony Wedgewood Benn (the then Minister of Technology) drives it off.
APRIL Dunstable Town Football Club in financial trouble again. There was fear of folding up.

Two primary schools open – Ardley Hill (Lowther Road) and Lancot (off Lancot Drive). Each cost £86,000 to build.

MAY Gypsies with their caravans parked in Green Lanes were terrorising the local people with demands for water and other resources.
Downside prefab site estate was sold for £158,000 (£18,588 per acre).
Met Station site at Drovers Way was sold to George Wimpey for £225,000.
JUNE National Gliding Championships were held at Dunstable.
Arthur Noon landlord of the *Spread Eagle* retired after being there for eighteen and a half years.
JULY Railway bridge at High Street North was demolished. It hadn't been used since 1965 and was built in 1869.
AUGUST A local motorist became the AA's 4 millionth member.
Former Mayor (1932–36) Alfred Cook died aged 80.
OCTOBER 1,850 manual workers off at Dunstable Vauxhall.
Dunstable Town on last legs and have to fold up, unless immediate funds were found.
NOVEMBER The *Rifle Volunteer*, West Street was demolished.
Hundreds of children sent home from Dunstable schools after teachers staged a half-day strike.
DECEMBER Dunstable Police Supt Horace Woods awarded MBE.

1970
JANUARY The Board of Trade put forward proposals for an air safety zone around Dunstable, which could have put the gliding club in jeopardy, but luckily for all the visitors that flock to the Downs, gliding at the club is still flourishing.
FEBRUARY Two local bookmakers were fined a total of £1,400 for evading betting duty.
St Katherine of Genoa Presbyterian Church at Katherine Drive is given its own minister, the Revd Keneth Graham.
An attempt by two men to snatch a £2,000 payroll from Lloyds Bank was foiled by a woman as she hung onto the brief case containing the money.
MARCH Another blizzard leaves a trail of chaos in the town.
Plans for speedway track at the Town football ground, Creasey Park, opposed by the Housing Committee of Dunstable Council.
There was chaos at the Downs 'Orange Pit' on Good Friday, fierce battles taking place for the oranges.
Well-known scrap dealer F. W. Carter died.
APRIL 2,500 workers at Dunstable Vauxhall laid off due to an unofficial strike by workers at the Ellesmere Port Plant. Dunstable was at a standstill.
Mrs Joyce Creasey died suddenly, she was the wife of the late Walter Creasey who died three years previous in 1967.
Town officials and the youth leader of Porz (one of Dunstable's twin towns in Germany) were disappointed that we could muster up only eight youths to visit their town, whereas they send between twenty-five and fifty of their youths to Dunstable on the Youth Exchange visit scheme.
MAY Mr George Brown (now Lord George Brown) former MP visited Northfields School amongst many hecklers.
JUNE David Madel (MP for South Beds) re-elected in the 1970 General Election. Results – David Madel (Con) 38,085; Gwilym Roberts (Lab) 33,107. The Liberal vote was 6,956, David's majority 4,978.
Well-known cycle shop owner Charlie Cole aged 70 won two classic races for Veteran Cyclists within the space of fourteen days since his 70th birthday. A 30 mile race at the National Championships and a 25 mile time trial in the Isle of Man.
JULY Vauxhall Motors' employees kept being laid off then called back.
AUGUST On the 29th of this month 1,600 employees of Vauxhall laid off again.
SEPTEMBER On 5 September yet another 350 Vauxhall employees laid off.
Well-known golfer Stewart Field professional at Dunstable Downs Golf Club for thirty-three years retired at the age of 64. Stewart was appointed professional to the South Beds Club when he was only 19 and at that time was the youngest golf professional in the country.
OCTOBER Well-known local dentist for thirty years William McIvor Glen died aged 57.
NOVEMBER The local Chamber of Trade withdrew their support for the Good Friday orange rolling.
DECEMBER When Eastern Electricity workers worked to rule electricity power cuts hit Dunstable and there were two-hour cuts in every section of the town.
The former Christ Church in Clifton Road and High Street South (used then as a warehouse for the College Christmas Cracker Co) caught fire and large numbers of toys including plastic cars, table tennis sets were either burned or badly damaged.
Council workers received a £2·50 per week wage increase, this added £17,000 to the Borough Council's annual wage bill.
On 16 December the *Windsock* at the bottom of the Downs opened.
During 1970 three Dunstable men all members of the Dunstable Downs Golf Club achieved their first ever 'hole in one' and they did this on their own course. They were – Pat Lucas (Han 3) at the 164 yard 18th, Robert Thomas (Han 18) at the 123 yard 9th, and Geoffrey Fox (Han 20) at the 167 yard 2nd. They were presented with tankards.

1971
JANUARY Dunstable Vauxhall produced more lorries per day than any other town in Europe. Up to 360 vehicles per day came off the lines; 6,000 were employed at the factory at that time which covered an area of 98 acres.
Local factory workers took time off from work to attend a demonstration against the proposed Industrial Relations Bill.
New branch of Lloyds Bank opened at the Eastgate branch in Station Road.
Dunstable postal workers on strike, this included fifty postmen.
On 11 January the *Spread Eagle*, High Street North closed down.
FEBRUARY On the 2nd of this month Dunstable changes to natural gas from the North Sea. New appliances installed in every home and factory and in fact every building that used gas.
The Key Club loses its special house and supper licence. The bar had to close at normal licensing hours. In March 1977 it is learnt that this club is being turned into a public house and the planners have been given the go-ahead from South Beds Council's south area plans committee.
Decimalisation comes to Dunstable, the changeover went very smoothly.
MARCH On the 31st of this month the Associated Portland Cement Marketing Co closed down their works in Houghton Road and production of cement was stopped two years after the company had spent £4½ million on installing a new second kiln.
JUNE Christine Truman (then Britain's top tennis star) opened Dunstable Lawn Tennis Club new courts at Downs Road.
JULY Four men were on attempted murder charge of a Dunstable policeman who was stabbed twice in the chest.

On 23 July Dunstable Grammar School (High Street North) closes to make way for Ashton Middle School. More than 300 boys moved to the Southern Campus Site by Caddington Turn (now known as Manshead School). The headmaster Mr L. P. Banfield also went with them and has been there ever since. The new school accommodates over 1,000 mixed pupils. The foundation of the Dunstable Grammar School was laid in 1887 and since then many famous people have been educated at the school including the late Gary Cooper famous Hollywood star of the 1940s and 1950s, Sam Kydd star of many films and television roles (and still going strong), and also a Premier of Pakistan. If you were an ex pupil of Dunstable Grammar, you were thought to be of a very high education indeed, this was no doubt due to the quality of masters that taught there and of the high discipline that was called for. (I took many photographs of the school teams and got to know the masters and boys very well. My shop premises have been opposite the school site since 1950.)

Former Grammar School master and organist of the Methodist Church, the Square for many years, Arthur Boskitt died at the age of 73. He had served on the staff of the school for thirty-nine years from 1920 to 1939.

AUGUST There was a row over the necessity of the Council spending £480 for half the Council members to go on a trip to Porz.

The Council spent £764 on repairs to the Priory Church clock. When the clock was given to the church in 1734 by a Mrs Jane Cart, she also gave £1 per year for its repair (she obviously did not take into consideration the inflation that we have been suffering over many years).

On 14 August Dunstable roads were turned into rivers after torrential rain. There was 4ft of water under the Church Street railway bridge.

On the 23rd of this month the new Barclays Bank opened in High Street North.

SEPTEMBER The new Southern Campus School and Dunstable Upper School (now known as Manshead School) opened. This is the school that took the former grammar school boys and is naturally a much larger school. There were pupils at this school in February 1977.

OCTOBER Traffic wardens came to Dunstable. (A parking fine in 1971 would have cost you £2, now it is £6.)

Douglas Rees takes over as Police Supt from Supt Derek Hart.

Three well-known local ladies Miss Sybil Wells, Miss Christine Truscott and Miss Nora Marshall retire as nurses and midwives after delivering 7,500 babies between them.

NOVEMBER Dunstable 'Aquaria' pet shop was wiped out by fire; hundreds of birds, fish and animals were either burnt or choked to death. £2,000 of damage was done and the owner was not insured. The fire started near a storage heater.

Soaring prices for houses – a property costing £5,800 in 1970 would cost you £8,350 in 1971, up almost 50 per cent over the previous year and you would have needed an income of at least £2,000 per year to buy one on mortgage.

The population of Dunstable rose to 31,828 in 1971.

There was a waiting list for colour televisions, dealers could not get sufficient, they were finding it difficult to cater for the staggering demand due mainly to restrictions of HP being lifted in a budget. (A happy note on which to end 1971.)

1972

FEBRUARY Thousands of workers were laid off and many more were put on a three-day week due to large cuts in electricity because of the miners' strike. Dunstable families sat in candle lit rooms and many had to do without a hot evening meal and had no television to watch. It was a very gloomy time indeed when those miners went on strike.

There were 522 people unemployed in the town with only 112 unfilled vacancies. Dunstable's worst ever employment crisis hits the over 45s because they were considered too old by many firms.

Local cycle shop owner and well known racing cyclist Charlie Cole aged 71 appeared on the BBC 2 programme *Seventy Plus*.

Shopkeepers in Church Street (south side) pleaded with the Council not to demolish them.

On 24 February the *Glider* (corner of Oldhill and Lowther Road) officially opened. (It actually opened on 11 February when the licence was first granted.)

MARCH On 1 March the *Old Sugar Loaf* closed to make way for extensive alterations by the new proprietors Schooner Inns. The alterations were only made inside the building, the outside to remain unaltered and the name to remain the same. (Mrs Joan Allen the proprietress had been there for twenty-two years.)

Luton Town footballer Chris Nicholl who lived in Dunstable was transferred to Aston Villa for £80,000. He said he was sorry to leave the town.

The unemployment figures rose to 651 out of work.

APRIL Former Mayor of Dunstable (1961–62) Percy James Melton died aged 64.

Bagshawe's announced closure of their factory in Church Street, the site being taken over by Thomas Tilling. 350 employees lost their jobs.

JUNE Houses kept going up in price: in March 1972 £10,000, in June this would cost £14,500 – a rise of £4,500 in three months.

First house on the Green Lane estate completed.

AUGUST Prince William of Gloucester opened the European Gliding Championship at Dunstable Downs.

SEPTEMBER Well-known local man Joseph James Tither (a founder member of Microwave Associates) died aged 44.

Trustee Savings Bank raided, thieves blasted the safe and escaped with £9,000.

Bill Garner who was sold by Dunstable Town to Bedford Town, also in the Southern League, for £500 in 1970, was transferred to first division club Chelsea for a fee of £100,000 after being bought and sold for various fees by other clubs.

OCTOBER Dunstable Rep produced their 100th production, it was *She Stoops to Conquer*.

Edward Street Congregational Church demolished.

Five paint sprayers at Chryslers factory in Boscombe Road brought the firm to a complete standstill, they stopped work after complaining about bad conditions.

NOVEMBER Vauxhall Motors Dunstable celebrate its 30th anniversary of coming to Dunstable in 1942.

A local company known as Lumo Cars changes its name to Tricentrol Cars (Dunstable) Ltd.

DECEMBER There was a slump in the numbers of doctors practising in the town.

1973

JANUARY There was controversy over the Quadrant clock which kept going wrong, some wanted it pulled down others wanted it to stay. It had been giving trouble for years.

One-day strike at A.C. Delco, Vauxhall and Chryslers.

Well-known Frederick Morgan Bancroft died aged 62. He was a former master of Dunstable Grammar School from 1937 to 1970 before retiring in 1970.

Ald Leslie Mair a former Mayor of the town (1970–71) retired from Weatherheads (formerly Cycles and Wireless and Arthur Chattell Ltd) where he had worked for forty years.

FEBRUARY Forged £1 notes were circulating in Dunstable.

Well known Reg Hayes former Dunstable and Beds CC Councillor and licensee of the *Waggon & Horses* died aged 59.

Dunstable man 23 year old Tony Garton creates a non-stop (except for a five-minute break every hour) organ playing record of seventy-five hours, he smashed the previous record by three hours.

MARCH Our local dentists treat people from all over the country. They came to Dunstable because dentists in their own areas refused to do the specialised NHS work such as new dentures, bridges and crowns that apparently Dunstable dentists were willing to do. One local dentist said he had treated patients from Cornwall and Lincoln.

On 10 March the *Forester's Arms* (Chapel Walk) closed down, now demolished.

Under age drinking in Dunstable reaches alarming proportions.

APRIL Fifty toolmakers out on a 24-hour strike at A.C. Delco.

VAT starts in Dunstable (and of course for the rest of the country also) and how the traders loved it and still do. (Don't believe that last statement. Author)

MAY Watney pubs run dry in the town due to a strike at the brewery (no not Whitbreads).

Mr John Leslie Collins Flint takes over from Mr C. E. Chambers as manager of the Midland Bank West Street.

JULY Dunstable Post Office had grave staff problems, only half the (normally sixty-one) postmen are working their deliveries in the disrupted town.

Average price of a house in Dunstable was £9,480.

Huge floods swept the town after a fierce thunderstorm.

£1 million order made by the Post Office for 609 TK trucks to be constructed at Dunstable Vauxhall.

Summer 1973 the California swimming pool closed down.

SEPTEMBER Thirteen families were under a threat of eviction from their houses in Dorchester Close because they were tied houses of the Watling Street Tool and Gauge Company which was shut down by its Sheffield based parent group Aurora Gears. The Council promised to help.

OCTOBER A local family Mr Derek Fowler, his wife and their three sons were killed in a road accident when the taxi they were travelling in was in collision with concrete beams that had fallen from a lorry (a tragic loss). The taxi driver was also killed.

DECEMBER Dunstable motorists queued at the post office for petrol coupons as the threat of rationing loomed nearer because of a general cut-back in oil supplies to this country (luckily it never came).

In Dunstable and the rest of the country firms went on a three-day week because of the Government's restrictions over the fuel crisis (those were very black days indeed) and many small local businesses were threatened.

On 18 December the *Old Railway* Hotel (bottom of Westfield Road) closed down.

On 18 December the *Chiltern* opened 300 yards further up from the *Railway* at the bottom of Chiltern Road on the old brewery site, at a cost of £121,000.

1974

JANUARY The year started off with local shops and businesses working in the dark and cold. Employers and employees were finding conditions almost impossible to work in, imagine yourself under a hairdryer and then all of a sudden the lights go out and your hair is still wet, well this was just one of the problems that Dunstable people (and the rest of the country) were trying to cope with.

New roundabout completed at the junction of West Street and Chiltern Road.

FEBRUARY Audi NSU, High Street South closed down, 137 employees made redundant.

Rt Hon Edward Heath 'Ted' (the then Prime Minister) visits Dunstable for the second time (the first time was in 1967).

George Best (the controversial soccer star) gives Dunstable Town a £20 cheque to help buy the club a new set of goal nets.

Keith Cheeseman managing director of a Luton building firm came on the Dunstable Town Football Club scene and bought 45,000 shares from Mr John Bain who was formerly on the board of the club.

MARCH David Madel (Con) MP holds South Beds in General Election.

Plans for a greyhound track at Creasey Park were given the cold shoulder after a petition with more than 250 signatures had been handed to the Council.

On 31 March Dunstable lost its Borough status and became part of South Beds District Council.

JUNE Dunstable Town spent £10,000 on new players. A mystery fire caused more than £5,000 of damage to the main stand at Dunstable Town's Creasey Park ground, it was a bitter blow just when things were looking up for the Town.

JULY Rt Hon Reginald Maudling Chancellor and Home Secretary opened the new extensions of Dunstable Conservative Club at a cost of around £50,000.

Former England centre forward Jeff Astle signed for Dunstable Town and there was talk of George Best signing also.

AUGUST George Best (one of the country's most colourful and controversial names in football) plays for Dunstable Town at Creasey Park against a Manchester United side attended by between 5,000 and 6,000 spectators.

SEPTEMBER The Revd Raymond Walters Dunstan takes over as Minister of the Methodist Church, The Square (he will also be the Superintendent of the Methodist Circuit).

A strike by ninety setters meant the whole of the 1,300 production staff being sent home at A.C. Delco.

OCTOBER David Madel back in Parliament again for his third year of office for South Beds in the General Election.

NOVEMBER A row of disused cottages in High Street North at the top of Capron Road were described as a 'damned disgrace to the town'.

DECEMBER Housewives queued for bread because of strike by major bakery workers.

Intruders entered Manshead School and killed dozens of animals kept in the environmental science animal shed. It was described as a 'bloodbath'.

1975

JANUARY The town will still have a Mayor under a group called the Dunstable Charter Trustees and South Beds District Council will be represented by its chairman.

A Dunstable teenager gave up his career to train for a gold medal at the 1976 Olympic Games but died before he could take part. He specialised in long distance running.

Dunstable bus travellers faced a massive 30 per cent increase in bus fares.

On 18 January the new Recreation Centre opened at a cost of £1 million. During the weekend over 15,000 people looked over it. It was opened by Olympic Gold Medallist Mary Peters, OBE and Major Simon Whitbread Lord Lieutenant of Bedfordshire.

Cross Paperware get warrant of Royal appointment, granted by the Queen.

FEBRUARY Changing facilities at the Recreation Centre swimming pool are most seriously inadequate. Talks were to be held with the architects.

Thieves caused £400 damage at a Dunstable builder's offices but only get away with 4p.

APRIL Protests from angry parents over new bus fares because Dunstable schoolchildren were having to pay double what they were.

New Maxi Vac take over from the broom for the town paths

Hang gliders flying again (after being banned by the Council in January) but with certain restrictions – not on Saturday or Sunday afternoons. Dunstable hang gliding started about eighteen months previous and had around sixty members.

JULY Local doctor cleared of manslaughter charges in abortion case.

The worst unemployment figures in Dunstable for fifteen years – 813 out of work 590 men and 223 women.

AUGUST Dunstable Town FC were worried about their finances as moves were made by the official receiver's office to look into the affairs of Keith Cheeseman (the then club chairman). The floodlights were removed from Creasey Park.

South Beds Council give go ahead for 180 houses at Spoondell Quarry (off Meadway) 25 acre site.

30,000 cigarettes stolen from local newsagents and tobacconists Lavells in West Street, two members of the gang kept the assistants talking while the third member went into the store-room and helped himself.

The so-called '500 years of Dunstable' celebrations took place, but they proved rather a flop on the ratepayers' money. The event seemed to lack organisation.

SEPTEMBER Ludun celebrates 25th anniversary.

Chairman of Dunstable Town Football Club arrested on fraud charge.

On 24 September the *Queen's Head*, St Mary's Street closed down.

Two people injured in two 'Statty' fair accidents.

OCTOBER George Best makes his second appearance playing for Dunstable, this time against Luton Town, the score was 1–1 this time 3,000 turned up to watch the game.

NOVEMBER Armed and masked men stole £196,000 from the Midland Bank, West Street, after holding one of the bank staff and his family hostages overnight.

1976

JANUARY The year started off with the worst gales in the town for many years, trees fell on cars, roofs came off, hundreds of television aerials and fences blown down. In fact you name anything that could have been blown down in Dunstable and it was, causing thousands of pounds worth of damage.

There were over 1,000 people out of work in Dunstable.

A Dunstable girl, 20-year-old Miss Janine Wilcocks, was one of the twelve finalists in the 'Miss Anglia TV' competition.

FEBRUARY The new 36 bus service meant a bus every 10 minutes for 20,000 peak time passengers on the Dunstable–Houghton Regis–Luton route.

A new hall was opened at the Baptist Church, West Street at a cost of £38,000 which had meant four years of hard saving.

MARCH The Dunstable Football Club pleaded for help from the South Beds Council.

APRIL Council promised football club another ground if theirs was used for housing.

Thirty canaries were let out or stolen from an aviary in the back garden of a Dunstable house.

A lion being delivered to Longleat in Wiltshire from Edinburgh Zoo (where it had been on loan for twelve months) stayed at the *Sugar Loaf* Hotel overnight (it was of course in its cage, I can personally vouch for that).

MAY Demolition of the 300ft chimney at APCM was started (the demolition work was completed in November 1976).

Sandra Fields aged 19 was elected Carnival Queen. The judging took place at a Carnival Ball held in Tiffany's. There were sixteen contestants.

Arthur Buck Dunstable & District Scout Commissioner retired. The position is now held by Mr 'Bob' Taylor.

The first town carnival for fourteen years was held and it was the biggest and best spectacular ever held in the town. It was opened by Ed 'Stewpot' Stewart Radio DJ.

JUNE Youth Club set up volunteer night watchmen because of vandalism and thefts.

Week after week during the months of May and June, Dunstable Football Club at Creasey Park were experiencing extreme difficulties in every respect. The manager Barry Fry was dissatisfied, the floodlights had been taken away, there was a threat of a housing estate being built on the ground and there were threats of players leaving. The new chairman was Bill Kitt a local businessman (a comment by the chairman was that 'he intended to make the club pay for itself and not run at a loss like it had been').

JULY Council house rents go up 50p per week.

The new Health Centre (now near the Priory Church) opened at a cost of £250,000 (the old one was in Kingsway).

Taxi rank moves from High Street North to new site in West Street. Taximen lose up to 75 per cent takings because this is not close to the High Street, bus stops and bingo crowds.

AUGUST Hang glider pilot broke both of his legs when he crashed to the ground at Dunstable Downs. It was the most serious accident to have happened there since the Dunstable Hang Gliding Club started in 1973.

Just one day after a small grocery store opened in west Dunstable, most of the owner's new stock and the inside of the shop were destroyed by fire.

A local blind man's white stick was stolen from the porch of his house.

SEPTEMBER Barry Fry Dunstable manager was sacked and replaced by former Luton Town defender John Moore.

OCTOBER The Old Contemptibles have their colours laid up by the newly reformed Dunstable Royal British Legion at a special service held at the Priory Church (the chairman of the new branch is Mr Stan Sinclair).

NOVEMBER Dunstable man won £12,000 on the football pools.

The Council decided that Creasey Park should not be used for houses.

DECEMBER A rather happy note to end 1976 on is that well-known 94 year old John 'Toddy' Sutcliffe was given a free pint of beer every day by the brewery of his local pub.

1977

JANUARY A former chairman of Dunstable Football Club jailed.

Mr Milton Hargreaves Clerk at the local magistrates for the past ten years received the OBE in the New Year's Honours list.

The Victoria Club opened their new extensions which cost £40,000. 800 members enjoy the privileges that the club offers.

The Woolwich Building Society opened a new branch in Dunstable.

It was estimated that 425,803 visited Dunstable Downs last year (1976) for picnicking and watching the gliding. (I wonder how the estimators could have been so exact with their figures?)

It was proposed by the Council's Environment Committee to move the West Street taxi rank to the Square, Dunstable.

Cross Paperware become part of the paper giants Bowaters in a £2¾ million deal. They will form part of the Consumer Packaging Division.

Residents were anxious as to how the 400ft cement works chimney would be demolished.

FEBRUARY Fifty buyers were involved in the purchase of a semi-detached house in Station Road which was put on the market by a local estate agent for the staggeringly low price of £6,500. The house was owned by the North West Thames Health Authority who fixed the price which was thousands of pounds less than it should have been.

Mr Eric Royce, former Mayor (1971–73), Alderman and Town Councillor for twenty-five years, died.

MARCH Union leader Hugh Scanlon visited Dunstable College on their annual prize-giving day and gave the students one of his speeches.

APRIL The European Weight Lifting Championships were held at the Queensway Hall and it was the biggest tournament held in England since the 1948 Olympics at Wembley. The championships were held over two days and were attended by more than eighty of Europe's strongest men.

DUNSTABLE

1952–1977

Snow scene – Whipsnade Road near golf club (note abandoned bus), 28 March 1952.

'Green Man', Chalk Hill, coach outing to Birmingham, 26 April 1952.

Pioneer Corinthians Football Club, 27 April 1952.

(The late) Ald T. Sandland, Mayor of Dunstable unveils War Memorial, Priory Meadow, 13 May 1952.

1952 – Whipsnade Zoo's 21st Birthday Film Stars' Garden Party

Ellis Powell (the then Mrs Dale of 'Mrs Dale's Diary') with 'Vali', 22 May 1952.

Ann Todd (film actress) hands the key to 'Vali', 22 May 1952.

Dinah 'Genevieve' Sheridan (film actress), 22 May 1952.

Maurice Denham (actor) and Kathleen Ryan (film actress), 22 May 1952.

Arthur Askey 'Big Hearted Arthur' (fifty years in show business and still going strong) with his daughter Anthea, 22 May 1952.

The famous Chimps' Tea Party, 22 May 1952. ⬇

Zulu warriors performing their war dance to the delight of all the spectators, 22 May 1952.

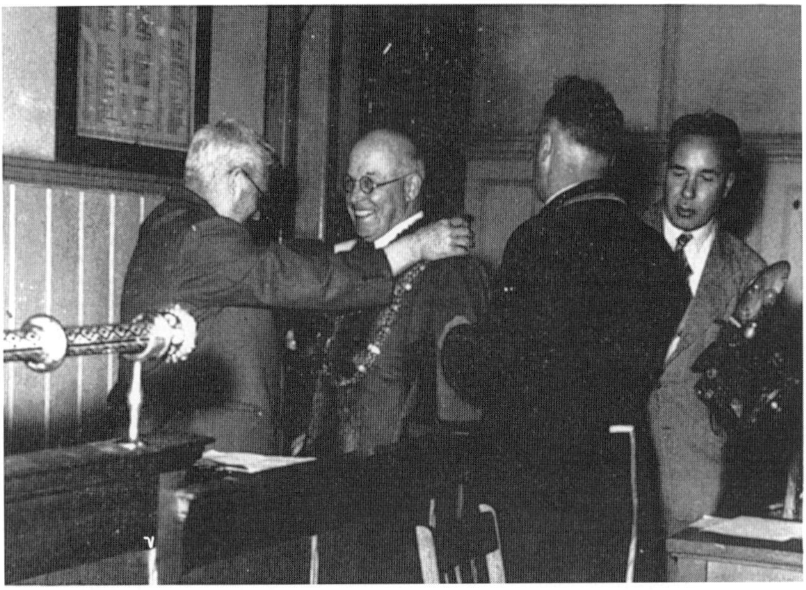

Ald T. Sandland puts the chains on the new Mayor, Ald B. J. Scott. (On the right can be seen George Gurney, the 'Luton News' and 'Gazette' staff photographer), 22 May 1952.

One of the last telegraph poles being pulled down in Dunstable High Street North, 4 June 1952.

Priory Church (West Front) and surrounds, June 1952.

Priory Church – same view showing wall gone and new layout, February 1977.

Meteorological station pylons from Totternhoe Road, July 1952. The meteorological forecasting station was based in Dunstable and moved to Bracknell, Berks. in July 1956 (the meteorological station Drovers Way site was sold to George Wimpey for £225,000).

The same viewpoint. Now Lancot Primary School, July 1975 (and as it looks today).

Downs Garage, Tring Road, July 1952.

The same viewpoint after alterations in July 1975, and as it looks today.

A.C. Sphinx (now A.C. Delco) tool room coach outing to London, 6 December 1952.

London Gliding Club Dinner Dance, 20 December 1952.

Confectionery Bazaar, 18 High Street North, February 1953.

Same viewpoint – Curry's electrical shop, February 1977.

Albion Garage, High Street North before being damaged by fire. 'The Towers', a large residence, can be seen on the extreme right, February 1953.

The same viewpoint after alterations following the fire which caused damage to the value of £3,000–£4,000, 12 December 1966.

A further change, now Albion Car Sales (renamed). Northgate Service Station can be seen extreme right on the old site of 'The Towers', July 1975 and as it can be seen today.

Victoria Street Coronation Street Party, 28 May 1953.

Half Moon Lane Coronation Party, 30 May 1953.

Half Moon Lane Coronation Party, 30 May 1953.

Westfield Road Coronation Street Party, 1 June 1953.

Kingsway – Coronation Party, 8 June 1953.

Worthington Road Coronation Street Party, 8 June 1953.

Worthington Road Coronation Street Party, 8 June 1953.

Beech Green Coronation Street Party, 15 June 1953.

Garden Road Coronation Street Party, 15 June 1953.

The 'Red Lion' High Street North with Coronation bunting. Closed down 17 March 1963 prior to being demolished for the Church Street road widening scheme. 2 June 1953.

The 'White Hart', High Street North with Coronation bunting, June 1953 (closed down July 1965).

Same viewpoint – Bejam and Halfords now in its place, February 1977.

The 'Winston Churchill', Church Street (opened 9 August 1965) which took the place of the 'White Hart'. The landlord and landlady, Jim and Betty McNamara left the 'White Hart' after being there for nearly three years and have been at the 'Winston Churchill' since. February 1977.

The 'Ewe & Lamb', West Street, June 1953 (closed down 19 August 1961).

Same viewpoint showing Chinese fish shop on the corner opposite the site where the 'Ewe & Lamb' stood, May 1974.

Same viewpoint – now being used as a car park, February 1977.

The new 'Ewe & Lamb', Luton Road (opened 22 August 1961), February 1977.

'Star & Garter', High Street South and the Old South Stores, June 1953.

Similar viewpoint showing old people's flats on right, February 1977.

The 'Greyhound', High Street South, June 1953.

The 'Greyhound' after alterations, February 1977.

Whipsiderry Café and Enterprise Printing Works, High Street North, June 1953.

Same viewpoint – Allder (optician), Central Café, Flemons & Marchant (chemists), February 1977.

Dunstable Commercial Hotel, West Street, June 1953.

Same viewpoint – Petersons, Ripolin, and Facit-Addo, February 1977.

California Pool quarry being filled in: note chalets of Meadway Hostel in background, 1953.

Same viewpoint – California car park with Pipers Croft replacing the chalets of Meadway Hostel, February 1977.

The 'Nag's Head' and Town Hall, High Street North, June 1953.

Same viewpoint February 1977. (Note well known character 'Darkie' in his paper kiosk. He has been a paper-seller in Dunstable for over thirty years since he retired from work in 1947. His exact age? Over 90!)

The 'Forester's Arms', Chapel Walk. This space now being used as a car park, June 1953. Closed March 1973.

Some of the 2,500 school-children who saw the film of the Coronation at Union Cinema, 17 June 1953.

The Labour Club Ladies' Darts Team pictured after the presentations at Dunstable Town Hall. They were the league winners of the Dunstable & District Ladies' Darts League 1952–53. (The Labour Club used to be situated in High Street North at the corner of Chiltern Road, and after several years the premises were taken over by the St John Ambulance Brigade as their local headquarters.) June 1953.

A Dunstable Cricket XI pictured before playing a Northamptonshire XI on Waterlow's sports ground, 21 June 1953.

The Priory cricket team, pictured at Cross & Co's ground, 12 August 1953.

A Northfields school party group. Mr Underwood the headmaster can be seen second left front row, 17 December 1953.

B. G. England, London Road, motor cycles, and garage, December 1953.

Similar viewpoint – now Tricentrol (Ford car dealers), February 1977.

The Tuck Shop and dis-used building in High Street North (next to Grammar School), December 1953.

Similar viewpoint. The dear old Tuck Shop served many Grammar School boys with their ice cream, etc. February 1977.

The Victory School of Dancing at the end of yet another concert (the principal, Miss Olivia Hunt can be seen extreme right with her pupils). Many local women will remember those good old days (I certainly do. B.T.). 1 April 1964.

The late Rt Hon Hugh Gaitskell, ex Chancellor of the Exchequer speaking at the Town Hall. He had only a very small audience, 16 May 1954.

1954 – *Mayor's Parade and Civic Service*

Fire chief Danes leads his men into the Priory Church, 30 May 1954.

The ATC arrive at the church, 30 May 1954.

Inspector John, leads the mace-bearer followed by the Mayor the late Ald W. H. Robinson, Jack Smith Town Clerk, with the Rev R. French of the Priory Church and members of the town council after attending the service at the church, May 1954.

The late 'Chum Dickins' leads the Old Contemptibles out of Church Street (note the 'White Horse' on the left centre of picture), 30 May 1954.

Similar viewpoint July 1975 and as it looks today.

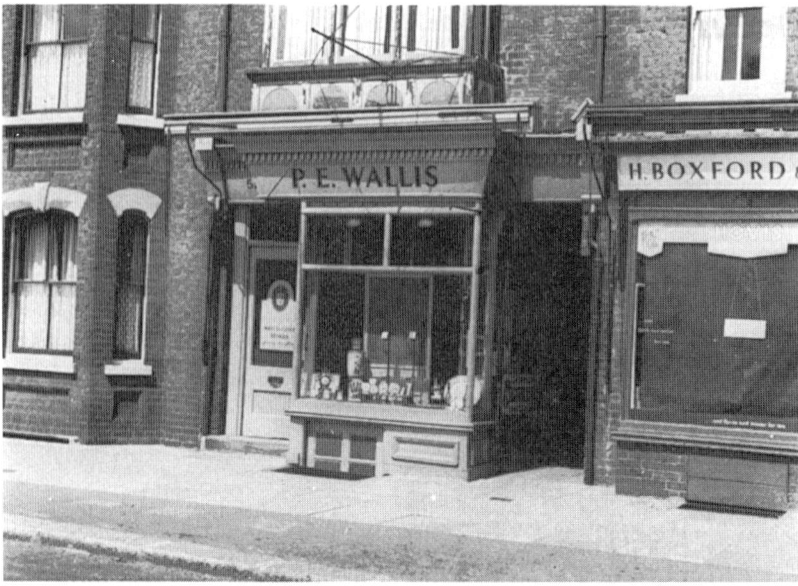

P. E. Wallis, antiques, Boxford, bakers, 51–53 High Street South, June 1954.

Same viewpoint – Allcorn Lockhart, estate agents, and Wisemans insurance brokers, February 1977.

A Guide group at the Priory Parish Hall, 11 June 1954.

A happy group of youngsters at the California swimming pool, 20 June 1954.

Criterion Café, and Gibbards corn merchants, High Street North, 26 June 1954.

Same viewpoint – Woolwich Building Society, and Palmers the estate agents, February 1977.

High Street North looking south towards centre of town. Behind the trees on the left was the residence called 'The Lawns' (the flags across the street were put up for the annual Old People's fete and carnival), June 1954.

Similar viewpoint – old Post Office extreme right and the new Post Office can be seen next to that. (I'll leave you to judge which view you like best: I know which I prefer. B.T.), February 1977.

Ladies' Captain's day at the Dunstable Downs Golf Club, 23 June 1954.

The California swimming pool, Whipsnade Road (at the bottom of Dunstable Downs), where I spent practically all my spare hours as a boy and in fact worked there for 1p (2½d) per hour, doing all kinds of jobs. These were happy days, now gone forever. I wonder if the pool will ever open again? (author). This picture was taken on a hot sunny day in June 1954.

Similar viewpoint – note the overgrown foliage. This picture taken July 1974. The pool finally closed in the summer of 1973.

The California car park in foreground – another viewpoint (the 'Windsock' can be seen centre of picture to the left), February 1977.

1954 – Old People's Carnival and Fete

Miss Phyllis Calvert (star of over fifty films) who opened the fete can be seen in the centre and to her right the late Ald W. H. Robinson, Mayor, and to her left Norman Cole, MP, 26 June 1954.

Miss Calvert gives her autograph to 4-year-old Rosemary Bliss, 26 June 1954.

Miss A.C. Delco contest at their 21st birthday celebrations. The winner was Miss Rose Sandle, presented with the sash by Miss Avis Scott, 3 September 1955.

Sea Cadets Christmas party, 10 December 1955.

Christ Church, High Street North, Guides' Christmas party, 16 December 1955.

Syntilla Manufacturing Co. dinner dance group at the 'Old Sugar Loaf', 16 December 1955.

Erg Resisters Christmas party at the Town Hall, 23 December 1955.

A.C. Delco motoring club dinner, held at the 'King's Arms', Berkhamsted, 10 November 1956.

Met Station dinner, held at the 'First & Last' Hotel, Church Street, 22 November 1956.

St John Ambulance Cadet party, 14 December 1956.

Albert Street off High Street South, 1957.

Same viewpoint with the Old People's flats, February 1977.

Grammar School rugby team, 2 April 1957.

Grammar School hockey team (the games master in both cases standing extreme left), 2 April 1957.

The Carnival Queen Mrs Elaine Rowe (in crinoline dress) and on her right Miss Wendy Phillips who was second; on Elaine's left, her sister Miss Joy Mead and Ann Patricia Warren (Miss Commer 1957) who tied for third place, 29 May 1957.

The 'Garratt' Cup teams and officials. Group photograph taken before the shoot-off at Bagshawe's. This was a competition for local clubs for small-bore rifle shooting, and was held annually, the last time this competition took place was several years ago in the early 1970s, 2 June 1957.

Dunstable Town cricket team at the town ground in Bull Pond Lane, 7 September 1957.

Waterlow's Ex-Servicemen's Association annual dinner at the 'Halfway House'. This association was disbanded in 1974, owing to diminishing membership. 28 March 1958.

Confirmation group with the Bishop at the Dunstable Catholic Church, West Street, 11 May 1958.

1958 Carnival Queen Contest

Line up of the entrants and seated the five judges (second left the late Mrs Joyce Creasey; centre Ald W. T. Lack, Mayor; extreme right Ald the late Walter Creasey, who later became Mayor in 1965), 12 June 1958.

The Mayor Ald W. T. Lack with the six finalists, 12 June 1958.

The winner (centre) Miss Joy Mead and her two attendants, on the left Miss Christine Cliff, and on the right Mrs Norma Strongman, 28 June 1958.

1958 – Carnival

Aberfeldy School float, 28 June 1958.

Part of the procession. (Note: shops in background to the right of Gas showrooms have now been demolished and the site taken over for Tesco's supermarket.) 28 June 1958.

The 'White Horse' Church Street (inset E. S. Reid the last landlord). The 'White Horse' was situated at the rear of the 'Red Lion' (see picture on page 18) and closed down on 4 March 1963. Picture taken July 1958.

The same viewpoint – the 'White Horse' was demolished to make way for this building and road widening. Alas another old pub gone forever, February 1977.

Kingsbury School first annual fete, 5 July 1958.

Yolande Pompey (former Empire and Commonwealth light heavyweight boxing titleholder) stops at Dunstable on his way back to London after knocking out Randolph Turpin in Birmingham, the previous evening, 10 September 1958.

High Street North, Albion Street to the crossroads, October 1958.

Similar viewpoint, February 1977.

The Dunstable Downs Golf Club clubhouse, 1958.

The clubhouse after alterations in 1974. Picture taken February 1977.

Dunstable Repertory Co.

Production of 'Running Riot' at the Town Hall, 20 October 1958.

Some of the cast in their production of the pantomime 'Alice-in-Wonderland' also at the Town Hall, 16 December 1958.

The rest of the cast in 'Alice-in-Wonderland', 16 December 1958.

'Have a Go' broadcast 'live' from Dunstable Town Hall with Wilfred Pickles, Mabel and the Dunstablians who took part in the show. Sitting at the table: left; F. J. Creak and on the right Wilfred Pickles. Standing at the back: left to right; Mabel ('at the table'), Mrs Ivy Williams, Miss Mary Gibbins, Mr Bill Goode, Mrs Phyllis Allen (who at that time had ten children) and Horace J. Darby, 13 January 1959.

Wilfred Pickles and his wife Mabel visit Kingsbury School, 13 January 1959.

New site and cross of St Augustine's Church, Downside, being hallowed by the Bishop of Bedford, the late Revd Basil Guy. The church was opened later in the year, in September 1959 and cost £10,000 to build. This picture taken 16 May 1959.

High Street North (top of Queensway) showing Anderson (outfitters), Barbers (hairdressers and chiropodist), and the trees of the house called 'The Lawns', May 1959.

The same viewpoint July 1975 (and as it is today).

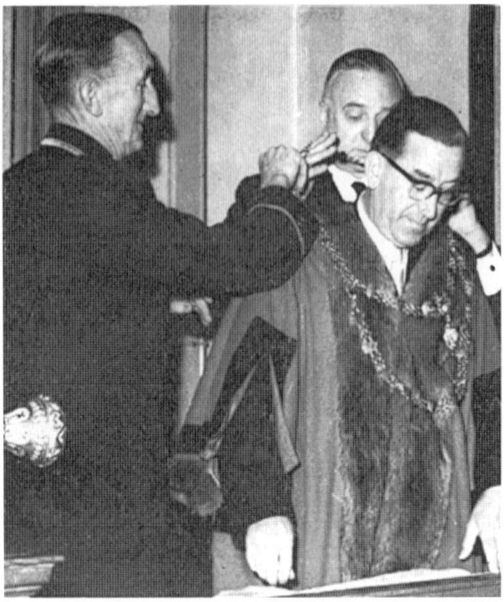

Ald L. Palmer becomes Mayor. Ald W. T. Lack hands over the chain of office, 19 May 1959.

One of the first production types of Lancer Boss side-loaders being assembled at the Syntilla Manufacturing Co, Luton Road. Lancer Boss later moved to large factory premises in Leighton Buzzard and since those early days at Syntilla Mfg, secured a £10 million contract with Allis Chalmer in America. Picture taken 14 August 1959.

A.C. Delco cricket teams, 19 August 1959.

The Rt Hon Harold Macmillan ('You have never had it so good') Prime Minister, seen arriving at the Square, Dunstable amid thousands of local people who turned up to hear him give one of his election speeches, 2 October 1959.

The PM seen delivering his speech; on his left seated, Mr H. Tawell past chairman of the South Beds Conservative Association, 2 October 1959.

Mr Macmillan seen with Norman Cole ex-MP for South Beds. Mr Cole was MP for South Beds for fourteen and a half years until he was defeated by Gwilym Roberts in the 1966 elections, 2 October 1959.

The cast of the Dunstable Repertory Company on the set of 'Johnny Belinda' at the Town Hall. The company later took over the old Library in High Street South and named it 'The Little Theatre' which opened on 5 October 1969. This picture was taken on 4 November 1959.

Meals-on-wheels service. On the left Mrs Edna Woods, on the right, Mrs 'Chippy' Chipperton. This was the first meals-on-wheels service run by the WVS and was made possible by the donation of this van by Vauxhall Motors Ltd. From 1948 to 1954 the meals-on-wheels service was run by the Dunstable Old People's Welfare Association. Later it was run by a small body of women until the WVS took over. With the use of this van, the work was entirely voluntary, and the service is still helping the aged and needy, 2 February 1960.

Mrs Woods and Mrs Chipperton serving Mrs E. Saunders, aged 73, with her hot roast, Yorkshire pudding, and potatoes, two vegetables, and sweet, 2 February 1960.

The opening of the California Ballroom by the Mayor Ald L. Palmer and Mrs Palmer Mayoress. On Mrs Palmer's right is E. W. Green who was the proprietor and who without employing contractors built the hall himself with the help of his family and friends, 2 March 1960.

Ronnie Carrol, well known vocalist, at the California Ballroom, 12 March 1960.

Commers (Dunstable) dinner dance at the 'Biscot Mill', Luton, 25 March 1960.

Ray Ellington and Valerie Simpson. Ray used to appear on the BBC radio programme called 'Roundabout' with the Ray Ellington Quartet. He also took part in 'The Goon Show', 16 April 1960.

Go-Kart racing at the California (next to the ballroom). Several meetings took place at the California and were organised by the Dunstable Kart Racing Club, but was finally discontinued because of the lack of attendances, Easter Monday 18 April 1960.

Clarke's hardware store and garden centre, High Street South (opposite Britain Street), 30 April 1960.

Same viewpoint – 1977 (rebuilding took place in 1963–64).

At Waterlow's 'Married' v 'Singles' football match. The married team, 6 May 1960.

The 'Singles' team, 6 May 1960.

The old almshouses at the corner of Ashton Street and West Street, 28 May 1960.

The same viewpoint, February 1977.

1960 Carnival

The Repertory float, 25 June 1960.

Part of the procession about to pass the cinema, 25 June 1960.

High Street North and centre of Dunstable looking south from top of cinema, July 1960.

The same viewpoint, February 1977.

Kenneth More (inset) and the rocket ship that 'took him to the moon' in the film 'Man in the Moon'. Picture taken during the shooting of the film at the APCM quarry top of Houghton Road, Dunstable, July 1960.

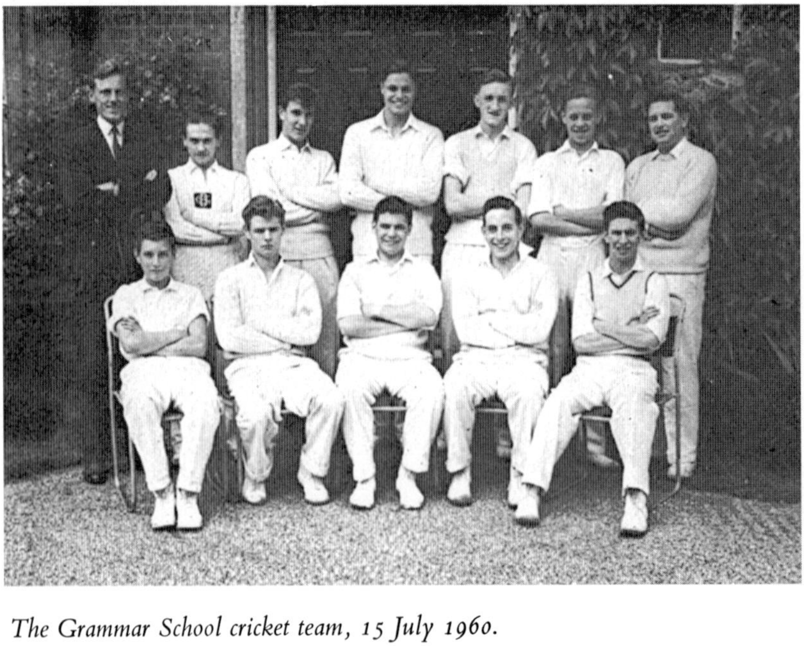

The Grammar School cricket team, 15 July 1960.

The bandstand, Grove House Gardens, 28 August 1960.

The same viewpoint, February 1977. (I wonder why it disappeared?)

New oil refinery, Brewers Hill Road, 25 September 1960.

Same spot (different viewpoint) – another Dunstable landmark bites the dust, 17 June 1975.

Beechwood House, top of West Street (bottom of Whipsnade Road), 1960.

Beechwood Court (same viewpoint) erected 1968 on the same site by Robinson & White. Picture taken February 1975 (and as it looks today).

Sam Costa, well known radio personality for such programmes as 'Much Binding in the Marsh' and for his regular DJ chat shows, seen at the Town Hall publicising records for the local music shop, November 1960.

Vauxhall Dunstable New Year's Eve party at the Dunstable canteen, 31 December 1960.

Sam Kydd, well known actor of many films and television parts including Mr Walton in 'Crossroads', and an Old Boy of Dunstable Grammar School, returns to his old school to open a fete, 18 March 1961.

Pioneer Corinthians Football Club pictured at their club headquarters at the 'Victoria', West Street (the landlord 'Ernie' Prutton fifth from left standing at the back), 3 May 1961.

High Street North, cinema to gas showrooms (showing part of the old cinema), 10 May 1961.

Similar viewpoint showing new shops and new post office, February 1977.

Mr J. J. Davis, works managing director of Associated Portland Cement Marketing Co, hands over the key to the Mayoress and the Mayor the late Cllr P. J. Melton, of the Olma Road Recreation Ground (2.89 acres). The company gave this to the council and charged them a nominal rent of 5p (1s) per week, 25 May 1961.

Grammar School cricket team, 19 July 1961.

Church Street towards centre of town from the Old Palace Lodge, September 1961.

Same viewpoint – after demolition of properties and road widening, July 1975 (and as it looks today).

Guild of Vergers annual meeting (held in a different town each year). Group taken outside Chew's House, High Street South. Left to right: Canon Mackonochie, Rector of Dunstable Priory; the Bishop of Bedford and W. G. Samways, then the verger of the Priory Church and secretary of the National Guild of Vergers, 12 September 1961.

Dunstable Vauxhall indoor games winners with their prizes at the indoor games presentation dinner, held at the Dunstable canteen, 24 March 1962.

Beecroft School football team, 12 April 1962.

The (old) 'Sportsman' (next to the garage on right), Winfield Street, 1962.

The same viewpoint, February 1977.

The (new) 'Sportsman', Katherine Drive, February 1977.

29 April 1962 – The Foundation Stone Ceremony of the New Catholic Church

The Mayor the late Cllr P. J. Melton (on his left) Father John O'Hare, following them Supt Horace Woods and Father Maurice O'Niel, arrive at the church.

The Bishop of Northampton, Leo Parker lays the stone.

The Bishop blesses the stone.

The Bishop reads the lesson.

Demolition of houses in Edward Street (corner of Regent Street), April 1962.

The same viewpoint – now old people's flats, February 1977.

Group of Sea Cadets with their trophies at their headquarters, the old mill (HMS 'Lionel Preston') West Street, 1 July 1962.

The Mayor Cllr Haydn Parrott with D. C. Earle Commanding Officer of the local unit inspects the ATC Cadets after a civic service held in the Priory Church. The ATC were celebrating their 21st birthday, 23 September 1962.

24 September 1962 – The 'Statty' fair comes to town

The scene when the Statute fair came to the Square every September. The fair is believed to have dated back to 1870 and under a Charter rules were drawn up by Dunstable local lovert board that the fair should come to Dunstable forever on the fourth Monday in every September, and up to now the Charter still stands but, alas, this scene can never be repeated as you can see from the photograph below taken after the town planners stepped in. There were stalls on the Square and stalls in side streets and nearby car parks. The Statute fair is now known as the 'Statty' fair. The fair this year (1977) will be held on the Queensway car park.

The same viewpoint, February 1977.

'Dave' showing off at the coconut shy.

No sign of fear here, 'The Octopus'.

30 November 1962 – Grammar School Rugby teams

The 1st XV.

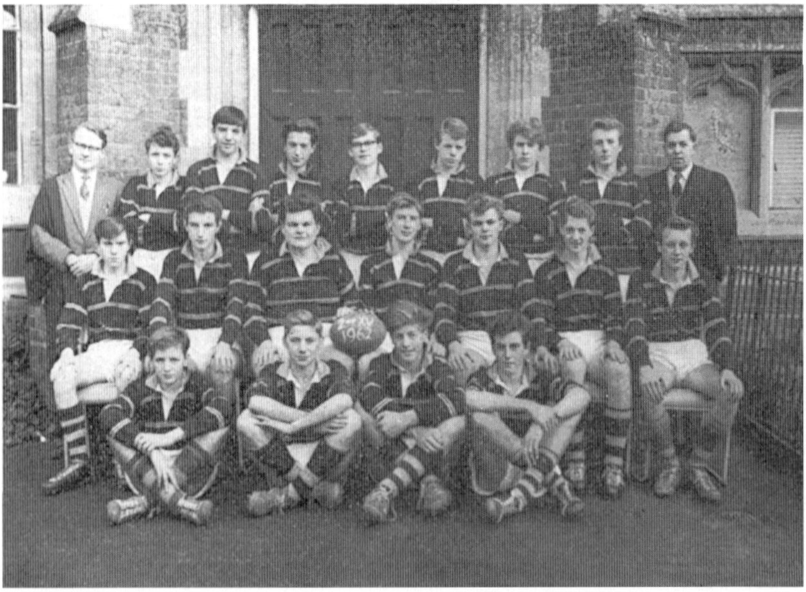

The 2nd XV.

A unique photograph of Dunstable (High Street North looking south). Not a person or vehicle in sight. It took $1\frac{1}{4}$ hours to take and I would say impossible to record now without police co-operation. The hands of the Town Hall clock were exactly at 3.00 pm the time of the Queen's speech. It was taken on Christmas Day 1962.

Seeing the new year in at the Vauxhall Dunstable Recreation Club's New Year's Eve party (a fitting end to 1962), 31 December 1962.

January 1963 – The Town Hall

The Town Hall was put up for auction in July 1965, but was withdrawn after bidding reached £41,000. The bid was made by a representative of Connells the auctioneers (but there were in fact two genuine bids of £30,000 and £32,000). The building remained unsold until a further auction took place later in the year in November when it was sold to the Pearl Assurance Co, for £35,000. The Town Hall was built in 1880 and was demolished in July 1966. (See aslo photograph on page 137.)

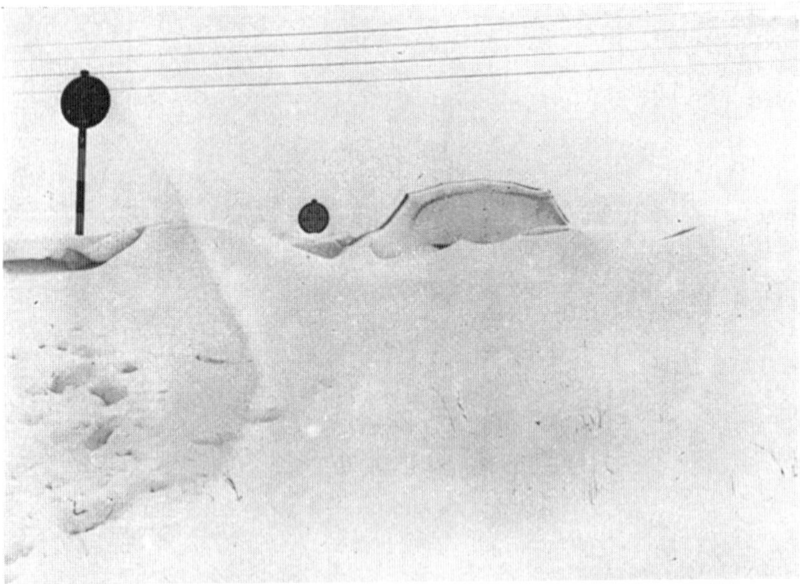

A 'no waiting' notice can just be seen above the 10ft of snow at the top of the Downs, Whipsnade Road, January 1963.

1962-63 – Winter

Looking towards Whipsnade (with Dunstable Downs golf course on left), January 1963.

This scene looking towards Dunstable. Both pictures are the Whipsnade Road. This sort of weather with bitter cold and continuous freezing continued for several months. A winter certainly for Dunstable to remember, January 1963.

Market stalls in High Street North where the old market used to be held (but no business this day). This market closed down and moved to its present site in Queensway in March 1964. Picture taken January 1963.

The new site, Queensway (Court Drive and Grove House gardens in background), February 1977.

High Street North (looking south), January 1963.

Similar viewpoint, February 1977.

Index Printers' dinner at the Halfway House, 5 January 1963.

Dunstable Women's Institute pantomime at the Town Hall, 29 January 1963.

Bedfordshire Boy Scouts Association County Cub 'Palavar' held at the Maltings, Nicholas Yard, High Street North. The County Commissioner Air Commodore J. E. R. Sowman is seen with local Cub Masters, 10 March 1963.

Armand Dennis (kneeling) well known television personality (for his wild-life programmes) seen inspecting copies of his 'wild-life' calendar coming off the new web offset machine at Waterlows who printed it for him. With him is the late Roland Todd, works manager, 10 April 1963.

Young Red Cross Cadets of 4910 Unit, Ashton Road, receiving their enrolment badges from the Commandant Mrs V. Bowerman, 13 May 1963.

Grammar School hockey team, 17 May 1963.

Ludun charity football match at Bagshawe's ground, staged by the Star & Garter Winkle Club – Under 40s v Over 40s. The veterans won. Group shows both teams, 2 June 1963.

Dunstable Young People's Club. Group of boys showing off the trophies they won at the Beds Association of Boys' Clubs' annual sports, 21 June 1963.

24 June 1963 The Pageant at the Priory Meadow

HRH The Duchess of Gloucester arrives at the Old Palace Lodge and is greeted by Major Simon Whitbread Lord Lieutenant of Bedfordshire, and the Mayor Ald M. Kilby. (Mr Kilby, at the age of 38, was the youngest person ever to be Mayor of Dunstable.)

The Duchess is greeted by the Mayor on her arrival at the Priory Meadow to open the Pageant, depicting the history of Dunstable over the last 750 years.

Four-year-old Nicola Smith on her way (under safe escort) to present the Duchess with this charming bouquet.

The 'Consecration of the Church' in 1213 re-enacted. Over 1,000 local performers took part in the Pageant watched by large crowds at every performance. 24 June 1963.

The 'Royal Oak', Church Street, before being demolished.

Similar viewpoint – now old people's flats, July 1975 (and as it is today).

The crossroads Dunstable where the A5 (London–Holyhead road) crosses the A505 road, Church Street and West Street. (The A5 is also known as the Watling Street and dates back to Roman times, and was in fact built by the Romans.) Photograph taken prior to the Church Street road widening scheme, 1963.

Similar viewpoint, February 1977.

7 July 1963 – Girls' Life Brigade Annual Parade

Forming up in Friars Walk.

The girls pass the Town Hall (note in background the Ace Café, Greens Stores and W. Hicks, tobacconist and confectionary). 7 July 1963.

Whipsnade crossroads crash, between Green Line bus and Standard 8 car (three people were killed in the car including one Dunstable person and two relatives). There have been many crashes at this spot and it has been one of the blackest spots in the area. 6 August 1963.

Grammar School choir, 20 December 1963.

Vauxhall Recreation Club's Christmas party at Dunstable canteen, December 1963.

'Workers' Playtime' broadcast 'live' from Commer Cars' factory canteen in Boscombe Road, Dunstable. Third from left Ann Shelton (vocalist), in centre Betty Smith (saxophonist) with Bill Gates (standing) the producer of the programme, and others who took part, 31 January 1964.

West Street (between Matthew Street and High Street). Shanks & Turner sports shop centre left, 10 February 1964.

Same viewpoint (note the new Midland Bank), February 1977.

March 1964 – Opening of the new Catholic Church

Councillors arriving in a snow storm.

The Bishop of Northampton, Leo Parker, unlocks the door of the church.

The scene inside the church. The church, which cost around £85,000 to build, was thought at the time to be the first circular church to be built in England for 400 years.

This group was photographed after the opening. Third left Father Maurice O'Niel, on his left the Bishop, and on his left the Mayor Ald M. Kilby, 15 March 1964.

16 April 1964 – The Opening of the Civic Hall (later renamed Queensway Hall)

The procession of the official party leaves Grove House (then used as the council offices) on their way to the Civic Hall, led by Police Superintendent Leslie Austin, the Town Clerk Jack Smith, the Rector of Dunstable Priory Canon Mackonochie, Sheriff G. S. Inglefield, the Lord Mayor's Mace-bearer, the Sword Bearer, and the Lord Mayor of London C. James Harman.

Some of the invited guests and VIPs including (sixth from left in the front row) M. Roger Courbatere Mayor of Brive La-Gaillarde in France (Brive is also one of Dunstable's twin towns and takes part in the youth exchange schemes). On the extreme right (seated in front row) is Lord Hill (who was also known to millions of radio listeners as 'The Radio Doctor').

The Lord Mayor of London C. James Harman unveils the Commemorative Plaque. (It is unusual for the Lord Mayor with his entourage to leave London.)

The official party seen in the Vernon Room of the Queensway Hall, 16 April 1964.

At the end of the Mayor's Centenary Civic Banquet and Ball held in the Civic Hall, 17 April 1964.

This chemical absorber was the longest (and possibly the largest) item ever to be manufactured in Dunstable. It measured 9in short of 100ft and weighed 37 tons. It was made for the ICI chemical plant near Bristol and left Dunstable by a specially constructed British Rail trailer: it was manufactured by the Syntilla Mfg Co, Luton Road, Dunstable. Syntilla Mfg closed down in 1969 and its plant, etc, was transferred to Blackpool to merge with BKP. Eighty workers were in protest at being kept in the dark and they were offered the chance to go to Blackpool. The old Syntilla site and factory is now being used by Ellis & Everard (Building Supplies) Ltd. Picture taken April 1964.

The old fire station to the right of Queensway (the new fire station is now at the bottom of Brewers Hill Road) 1964.

The same view, February 1977.

Kathy Kirby at the California Ballroom. (Kathy starred in the television show 'Stars & Garters' and also made the hit record 'Secret Love'.) 16 May 1964.

Seamus Dunne (seated), former Luton Town full-back, signs for Dunstable Town as new player manager, also in the photograph (standing) left to right: A. Thompson, director; J. C. Bain, vice-chairman; Sid Smith, match secretary; W. T. Lack, director and chairman of Supporters' Club; (the late) Ald Walter Creasey, chairman; and Harold Stew, secretary (and still is). Seamus was sacked in 1968 after being manager for four years. 31 May 1964.

The 'Rifleman' darts team pictured at the 'Biscot Mill', Luton after being presented with the league cup and league knockout shield which they won in the 1963–64 Mann Crossman Dunstable & District Darts League. (The captain Steve Brodie is seen holding the shield, and the landlord Tommy Varle seen holding the cup.) 10 June 1964.

These ten Kingsbury School boys are seen after being presented with their Duke of Edinburgh Bronze awards, which they received from the Mayor Ald Leslie Worby. Also in the picture is the headmaster, Mr S. Robinson. 16 July 1964.

Sir Alec Douglas Home visits Dunstable

Sir Alec Douglas Home (now Lord Home) Prime Minister, seen at the Square delivering his speech during an election campaign. (Norman Cole now ex-MP is seen bottom right-hand corner.)

This was the scene on the Square, 7 October 1964.

How many of the locals recognise faces in these two crowd scenes? 7 October 1964.

American singer Brenda Lee at the California Ballroom, 4 December 1964.

Dunstable Vauxhall St John Ambulance awards, 20 February 1965.

Local heavyweight boxer Cliff Field being presented with his trophy from Harry Carpenter (well known BBC radio and television sports commentator) after winning the Combined Services Championships and quarter final of the ABA championships at Stanmore, Middlesex. Picture taken 1 April 1965.

'Too many cooks spoil the broth': these young ladies were performing in the Victory School of Dancing concert held at Kingsbury School, 26 May 1965.

This group of children are seen with Father O'Niel after attending first communion at the Catholic Church, 21 June 1965.

The APCM bowls team, 28 September 1965.

Mrs Hislop's keep fit ladies at Kingsbury School, 31 January 1966.

Jimmy Tarbuck (well known comedian and television star) seen at the ABC Cinema in the projection room with Arthur Frost, assistant projectionist, 15 March 1966.

Prime Minister Sir Harold Wilson seen at the Queensway Hall on his election campaign. On his right is Gwilym Roberts ex-MP for South Beds and now MP for Cannock; there was a noisy reception for the PM from plenty of hecklers. 24 March 1966.

The cement works chimneys at Houghton Road were a Dunstable landmark that could be seen for miles around. The taller (400 ft) chimney was added when the APCM installed another kiln. The whole installation being completed in 1969 at a cost of £4½ million. This trebled the production but only carried on for two years when production was stopped on 31 March 1971, and no further cement was produced. Picture taken on completion of the 400 ft chimney, 28 April 1966.

One down . . . one to go

The smaller 300 ft chimney disappeared in 1976 (and by the time this book is published the larger 400 ft one will probably be gone as well). The site is still being used, but only as a distribution centre for cement. Picture taken February 1977.

June 1966 – Quadrant Shopping Centre Opens

Bob Monkhouse (well known comedian, film and television star in programmes such as 'The Golden Shot' and 'Celebrity Squares') declares the Quadrant open. On the left of photograph the Mayor Cllr C. W. A. Conway, and the Town Crier of Warwick, Henry Thistleton (as Dunstable had no Town Crier). Bob arrived late for the opening due to the immense crowds. 3 June 1966.

The Town Hall being demolished (see also photograph on page 106), July 1966.

The Dunstable College float, 1966 Carnival, 26 June 1966.

Guides Swimming Gala Group, Kingsbury School, 1 July 1966.

St John Ambulance Demonstration

The St John Ambulance Brigade seen 'rescuing and helping' the injured at the scene of a demonstration rail crash at the Dunstable North Station. The station was demolished in January 1967 following its closure for passenger services on 24 April 1964. These pictures taken 10 July 1966.

Scene on the platform of the station, 10 July 1966.

Group of apprentices at Syntilla Manufacturing, Luton Road, 8 December 1966.

The 'Barron Knights' well known pop group of Dunstable and Leighton Buzzard boys. The group has made several records and appeared all over the world (including the London Palladium). Dunstable lad Richard Palmer (Duke D'Mond) can be seen in the centre of photograph, another Dunstable lad Tony Avern acts as their manager (not in the photograph). Picture taken at the Lea West Bowling lanes, Cesars Palace. (The bowling lanes closed down and the building is now being used as a Bingo hall.)

1967 – Rt Hon Edward Heath visits Dunstable

Mr Edward Heath being greeted on his arrival by David Madel, MP for South Beds.

Chatting to constituents in the Quadrant shopping centre.

Speaking to members of the Conservative Party at the 'Old Sugar Loaf'.

Enjoying 'a cuppa' after his press conference at the 'Old Palace Lodge'. (An exclusive picture just for the author) 18 November 1967.

The opening of the new Pearl Assurance Co Ltd offices on the site of the old Town Hall, High Street North (they purchased the Town Hall and site for £35,000 in November 1965). 30 November 1967.

Raymond Baxter (well known radio and television commentator also of the 'To-morrow's World' programme) seen with members of the 'Mini 7' Club when he gave them a lecture at the 'Saracen's Head', High Street South, 16 April 1968.

Borough Arms football team, pictured at the town ground before they played a team from Jersey, 11 August 1968.

5 September 1968 – Empire Rubber Co, Wages Snatch

Empire Rubber Co. £11,000 wages snatched. 5 September 1968.

The Mayor Ald P. N. Wainwright, handing over the shield at the granting of the Freedom of the Borough, to Major Lisle Orchard commanding officer of the battalion (the then major now holds the rank of colonel). On the Mayor's right, Leslie Rallison, Town Clerk, and on his right, Major Simon Whitbread, Lord Lieutenant of Bedfordshire.

The Mayor's Macebearer George Gage, leads the Mayor and the Major at the inspection.

The general scene of the Queensway car park taken from the Queensway Hall.

The Mayor takes the salute at the march past in Court Drive, 13 October 1968.

Waterlow's Automation Services' 'Personality Girl' contest at the Bossard Hall, Leighton Buzzard. The winner was No 1, 18-year-old Miss Carol Clarke. 25 October 1968.

The 'Scrumbumblers' Rave Up! at the Old Sugar Loaf. The 'Scrumbumblers' were formed by local ex-rugger lads and are all very well known in the area, four Newmarket jockeys attended this function, M. L. 'Taffy' Thomas, 'Kipper' Lynch, Greville Starkey, and Eric Eldin (seen in the middle with his arms wide apart). On the floor extreme left (with his right arm in the air) is 'Billy' Watts son of the Queen's racing trainer. 30 October 1968.

The 'Rifle Volunteer', West Street, being demolished, October 1969.

The same viewpoint the 'Windsock' on the site of the 'Rifle Volunteer' (this is at the bottom of the Downs, Whipsnade Road). The 'Windsock's high roof has not stood up too well to the severe gales that Dunstable has suffered over the past few years, and this gave cause for some concern. July 1975 and as it looks today.

The Pioneer Corinthians football team, Bennetts Recreation Ground, 21 March 1970.

Reg Young who was a well known Dunstable bookmaker seen at the White City Stadium, London, receiving the Greyhound Derby Trophy from the Earl of Westmorland, after his dog, 'John Silver' had won the 1970 Greyhound Derby. 'John Silver' at twenty-two months was the youngest dog ever to win the Greyhound Derby and appears in the 'Guinness Book of Records'. It still holds this record. Reg, who besides owning the dog also bred it, and now breeds, owns, trains, and runs greyhounds all over the country. 27 June 1970.

New Year's Eve at the United Services Club, 31 December 1970.

Brewer's Hill School rugby team (1970–71), 29 April 1971.

The Old Sugar Loaf prior to alterations, 1972

The reception area.

The banqueting hall.

The lounge bar.

Looking towards reception area from lounge bar, January 1972.

Opening of the Vauxhall Recreation Club's new lounge bar, 2 May 1972.

Councillors and officials from Brive in France (one of our twin towns) with councillors and officials from Dunstable, at the 'Old Palace Lodge', 17 May 1972.

Dunstable Town cricket team, 5 July 1972.

The Mayor (the late) Ald Eric Royce, seen with young visitors from Brive, in the Grove House Gardens, 18 August 1972.

Prince William of Gloucester at the opening of the European Gliding Championships held at the London Gliding Club, Dunstable. With the Mayor (the late) Ald Eric Royce, and John Jeffereys manager and chief instructor of the club. (The prince was killed in an air crash less than 24 hours after this 'exclusive' photograph was taken.) 19 August 1972.

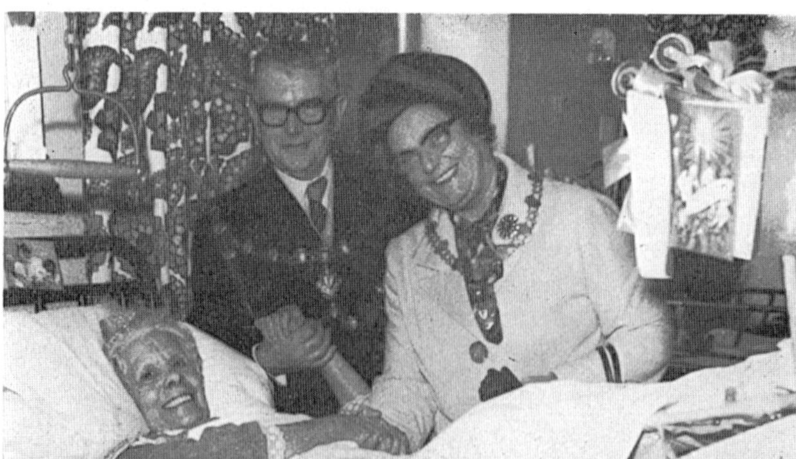

The Mayor and Mayoress (the late) Ald Eric Royce, and Mrs Royce seen with Mrs May Cox of Dunstable, in the Luton & Dunstable Hospital, on Christmas Day (this is when the Mayor and Mayoress of both Luton and Dunstable visit the hospital and chat to patients). Mrs Cox was recovering in hospital after being pinned under a lorry in Union Street. 25 December 1972.

Dunstable firemen on duty Christmas Day, just after their Christmas dinner (which they cooked themselves), 25 December 1972.

Fred Davis (Joe's brother) ex world snooker champion left; Jimmy McCrystal (Vauxhall Dunstable snooker player) centre; Rex Williams professional snooker champion and ex world billiards champion; and in background, Sidney Lee BBC 2 'Pot Black' referee, seen at Vauxhall Dunstable after giving an exhibition of snooker, billiards, and trick shots to a packed recreation club. 30 January 1973.

'Corner House' corner of Totternhoe Road and Tring Road, prior to being demolished. 22 February 1973.

The same view, now maisonettes July 1975 and as it looks today.

Wrestling at the Queensway

'Wrestling' at the Queensway Hall – just one of the many contests staged to capacity crowds at the hall; a number have been televised. In the photograph Zoltan Boscik pins Vic Faulkner to the floor. 28 February 1973.

Kent Walton (television commentator and personality) seen commentating for ATV, 28 February 1973.

Dunstable Bowling Club's new rinks open at Hawthorn Close. The Dunstable Bowlers seen above. 28 April 1973.

Dunstable Town cricket team on the Bull Pond Lane ground, 28 April 1973.

Old cottages in West Street being demolished, May 1973.

The same viewpoint showing the old and the new Catholic churches, and the new car park, February 1977.

The front of the old Catholic church (1959).

The old church showing new look (and now used as the Catholic Social Club) and the new church, February 1977.

The Conservative Club, High Street North before extensive alterations, May 1973.

The club (which now has a membership of 800), after alterations, February 1977.

Northfields School under-15s footballers, 4 October 1973.

Eighty years' service between these four Dunstable Firemen who were presented with long service medals for each completing twenty years' service. Left to right: Leading Fireman Mann, and Bert Linney, Fireman Fred Lander, and 'Topper' Baine, 2 November 1973.

November 1973 – Sunday Market

This open air 'Sunday Market' at Wellhead (opposite the Gliding Club) was the first market of this type to be held locally. It proved quite a success for the customers and stallholders but it was not too popular with the local residents who complained because of the long queues of cars. Between 15,000 and 20,000 people attended the market which was run by over fifty stallholders. The conditions were very bad however, with bad parking facilities and thick mud in which many cars got stuck. A large field was used for the purpose and there was some controversy as to who gave permission for the market to be held there, and there was an action by the Luton Rural District Council which ended up with over fifty stallholders being fined £5 each for illegally selling goods on a Sunday, as their stalls were classed as shops. As some of them said 'shops do open Sundays'. And so it just died a 'death' and there have been no more open markets there since. 25 November 1973.

Yet another crash at these ridiculous crossroads of ours. When will something be done? Picture taken 1973.

The Rt Hon 'Ted' Heath (the PM) visits Dunstable Conservative Club. Mr Heath is about to sign the visitors' book with the club chairman E. B. Trotman, 12 February 1974.

Another exclusive photograph of Mr Heath, seen with a painting of the late Sir Winston Churchill, 12 February 1974.

The Prime Minister seen with officials of the club including second left, E. B. Preater, Past President of the club. In the centre David Madel, MP, on his left Mr G. McIntosh, club Secretary and on his left Mrs Madel.

Bruce Benson, former DJ of the 'pirate' radio station 'Radio Caroline', performing at the California. Bruce is now a well known DJ throughout the area and also internationally. He was also one of the first proved DJs in Dunstable. He took on another new role in Dunstable as manager of the California in February 1977 (picture taken 30 March 1974).

31 March 1974 – End of Borough Status
Town becomes part of South Bedfordshire

End of Borough celebrations. Dunstable loses its borough status and becomes part of South Beds District Council. The Mayor Ald W. Farbon, the Town Clerk Miss P. Radge and Councillors leave the Priory Church after the civic service.

The Mayor outside the Queensway Hall seen receiving and thanking those that took part in the parade. 31 March 1974.

The trumpeters of the 'Blues and Royals' who took part in the various displays of marching, etc, on the Queensway car park, 31 March 1974.

This unique group photograph shows eleven past Mayors of the Borough of Dunstable. (Back row standing) left to right: the Macebearer Stan Sinclair, Ald P. N. Wainwright, Ald L. Palmer, Ald R. Wyles, Ald L. Worby. (Front row) left to right: Cllr W. Conway, Ald B. J. Scott, Ald L. Mair, Ald W. Farbon (the last Borough of Dunstable Mayor), Ald W. Lack, OBE, (the late) Ald E. Royce and Ald W. Allen. Note: the Mayors of Dunstable are now Mayors of the Charter Trustees. 31 March 1974.

This group shows the last Mayor of the Borough of Dunstable (standing on the right, front row) Ald W. Farbon, together with officials and long serving employees of the old Council. In the front row, on the left, Miss P. Radge the last Town Clerk, (on her left) Ald L. Palmer, who served over twenty-five years as a councillor, (on his left) Miss Marjorie Field, Secretary to the Town Clerk, and seventeen past Mayors of the Borough. In the centre of the group we have Harold Stew, Public Health Inspector, and (standing at the back extreme left) is Leslie Rallison, a former Town Clerk. 31 March 1974.

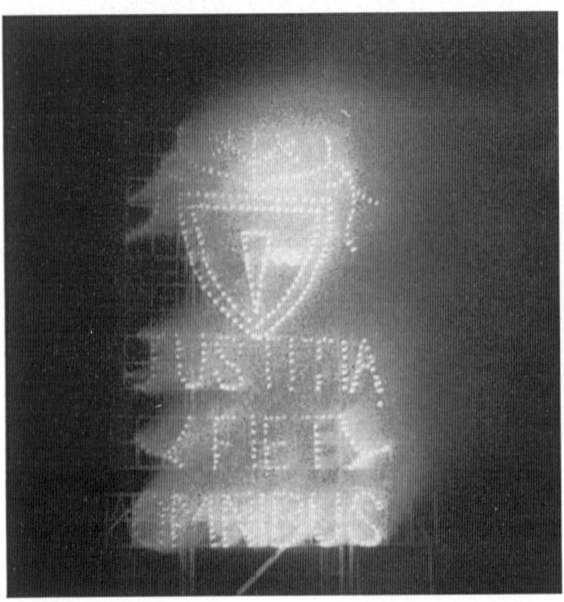

'The end of an era': the Dunstable borough crest burns itself out and the town becomes part of South Beds District Council, 110 years after the borough council was formed in 1864. Many other boroughs all over the country were wiped out overnight on the last day of March 1974.

The Dunstable Town Supporters' Club team who won the Whitbread-Rothmans Sports Quiz Final at the Hatters' Club, Luton, seen with soccer star Alan Ball (centre) ex-Arsenal and an England international, after he had presented them with their prizes. May 1974.

The Chiltern Singers, seen at Ashton Middle School, High Street North. This group of singers was formed with some of the nucleus of the old Dunstable Girls choir which was disbanded in April 1972. Photographed 17 July 1974.

The Rt Hon Reginald Maudling (a former Chancellor of the Exchequer and Home Secretary) unveils the plaque in the Dunstable Conservative Club at the opening of their new extensions, watched by past club chairman Mr E. B. Trotman. July 1974.

Mr Maudling pulls the first pint watched by some of the club members. July 1974.

Group shows David Madel, MP for South Beds, Mr Maudling, the Mayor of Dunstable E. S. Clark and Mr Trotman. July 1974.

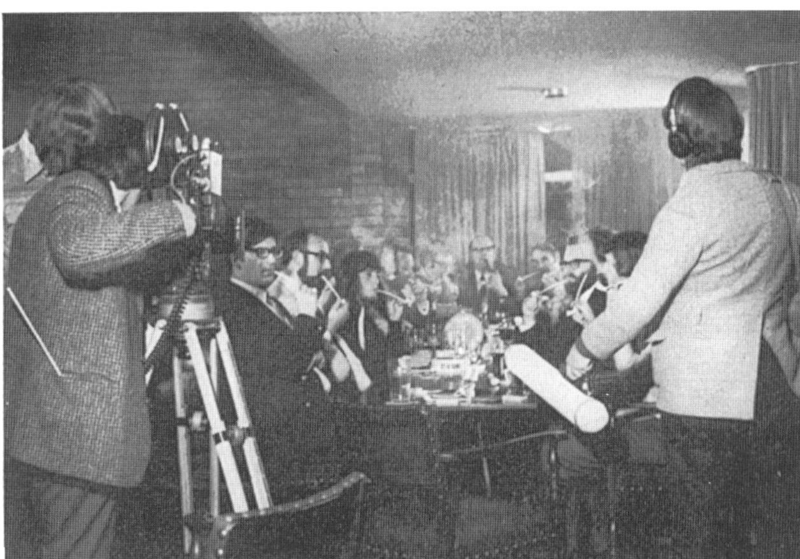

The Dunstable Pipe Smoking Club seen at the 'Chiltern' High Street North being filmed for the BBC television programme 'Nationwide'. They used 9-in clay Churchwarden pipes and they had five minutes to fill the pipe. They were given a short while to light up from one box of matches each, and then a contest started in which each competitor had to keep his pipe alight for as long as possible (if the pipe went out they automatically dropped from the contest). The winner kept his pipe alight 45 minutes (the British record is 2 hours 15 minutes and 50 seconds), 1974.

George Best (with beard) one of the most colourful and controversial names in football, visits and plays for Dunstable Town. August 1974.

George poses for a team photograph with Dunstable Town, before they played a Manchester United team. The chairman at that time, Keith Cheeseman, arranged and paid for Best to appear. August 1974.

Some of the vast crowd that attended the Town ground (the largest attendance ever recorded at the Brewers Hill Ground) to watch the star in action. The Dunstable Town ground was renamed 'Creasey Park' on 28 August 1967 in memory of the late Walter Creasey. A plaque was unveiled by Mrs Joyce Creasey. (He was known to everyone as 'Wally'.)

George watches recorded highlights of the game on television in the Boardroom after the match the same evening. On the left is club chairman Keith Cheeseman. (Cheeseman was sent to jail for six years in January 1977 for fraud and the embezzlement of £287,000. He was called 'A master swindler'.) Cheeseman took over the Dunstable Town Football Club in February 1974 and quit the club later in 1975. Photographed August 1974.

Margot Bryant, better known to millions as 'Minnie Caldwell' of the television serial 'Coronation Street' seen after she opened Bingo sessions at Tiffanys in the Quadrant, 14 September 1974.

Mary Peters, OBE and Olympic Gold Medallist (with Major Simon Whitbread, Lord Lieutenant of Bedfordshire) unveils the plaque at the opening of the £1 million Recreation Centre in Court Drive, 18 January 1975.

Mary keeps in trim in the leisure conditioning room. 18 January 1975.

Mary, the Lord Lieutenant and Mr J. McLaney (chairman of South Beds District Council) seen in the solarium. At one time the new centre was reported to cost £200,000 per year to run, with only an annual turnover of £100,000. 18 January 1975.

The official party seen on the steps of the swimming pool, 18 January 1975.

Some of the guests who attended the opening of the Recreation Centre, 18 January 1975.

Dunstable Town football team on the Town ground, with Keith Cheeseman in the centre. (In 1976 Dunstable Town Football Club changed its name and is now known as Dunstable Football Club.) 28 April 1975.

Margaret Powell well-known broadcaster and writer opening the Glenwood School (for mentally handicapped children) annual fete. The head teacher Margaret Keyte, is on the left. 15 June 1975.

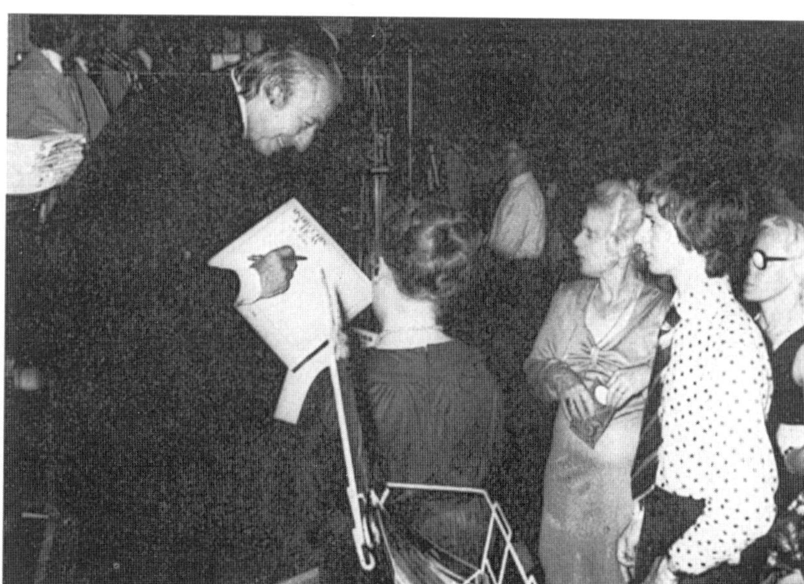

Joe Loss well-known bandleader and broadcaster, at Tiffanys night club, signing one of his records for a fan, 30 July 1975.

Flinte House, High Street North, corner of Ashton Street, July 1975.

Similar viewpoint, February 1977.

The Co-op car park adjoining Queensway; view from top of the Bingo hall, July 1975.

The same viewpoint with the car park now closed. The site is awaiting development by the owners, the Luton Co-operative Society. It was only temporarily on loan from the owners for use as a free car park. Just for the record all car parking in Dunstable is free. (I wonder how many towns can boast this?) February 1977.

'25 years of Ludun' – a non profit making firm that employs only disabled personnel. It is situated in Liscombe Road, which is off Luton Road, Dunstable. Ludun was the collective idea of three people: Mr Lawrence Plewes (who is now chairman of the directors), Dr John Rogers and Dr Brian Shaw. They were concerned about the welfare of disabled people at work, and in 1950 they formed Ludun in a mortuary building in Luton, with one of the main products being the leather boots that fit over plaster casts. The firm moved to a new factory in Liscombe Road, which was opened by the Duke of Edinburgh in May 1956. The picture taken at the factory shows the entire staff. Fourth from left is Mr Plewes, and ninth from left is Mr Leonard Hopkins who has worked for the firm since it started, and was presented with a long service award for twenty-five years. Photograph taken August 1975.

The '500 Years of Dunstable' carnival. No one seemed to know what was being celebrated as Dunstable had been going for nearly 900 years, and no one could say what happened in Dunstable around 500 years ago. The carnival proved to be a complete flop with excuses being made all round, and the parade took only about 3 minutes to pass (and as I stated in the local press, if you blinked or turned your head you could have missed it: perhaps a little exaggerated, but I think it sums it up). 22 August 1975.

The Mayor of Dunstable (the first *Charter Trustee Mayor) Mrs Pat Pocknell lays her wreath at the war memorial in Priory Meadow on Remembrance Sunday, 9 November 1975.*

The Luton Boys' Brigade sound the 'Last Post', 9 November 1975.

The 'Queen's Head' St Mary's Street, which closed 24 September 1975 – now demolished. The site is now an open space. 1975.

Midland Bank raid of £196,000. Four armed and masked men held at gunpoint the bank accountant and his family in their home near Dunstable all night, before taking him to the bank the next morning and forcing him to open the vault. They escaped with nearly £200,000. Photograph taken shortly after the raid on 26 November 1975.

David Kossoff, well-known broadcaster of his bible stories, and television personality, seen at the Methodist Church, The Square, signing the visitors' book prior to giving a lecture to a packed church. Also seen in the picture: Fred Moore treasurer (left); the Minister Rev R. Walters Dunstan and Peter Arminger (senior church steward), 27 November 1975.

Sea Cadets pictured at their ship HMS 'Lionel Preston' (The Old Mill), West Street after being presented with the annual awards, 28 January 1976.

The 1st Dunstable Allen Cub Pack (Brewers Hill) showing off their handicrafts which won them top award in the Dunstable and District Club handicraft exhibition, 1 February 1976. They came second in 1974 and 1975.

This fine group of women was taken at the Ladies' Keep Fit Rally in the Queensway Hall, 20 March 1976.

A scene from Dunstable Operatic Society's production of 'White Horse Inn', Queensway Hall, 23 March 1976.

A new sport 'hang gliding' comes to Dunstable Downs. Considered very dangerous in certain quarters as some pilots have been killed or badly injured. A council ban was put on hang gliding at Dunstable in January 1976 but in April of that year it was back again but not Saturday or Sunday afternoons. Dunstable Hang Gliding Club started at the end of 1963 and has about sixty members. At the time of going to press the sport seems to be thriving again and as many as thirty or forty hang gliders can be seen on the Downs (above the London Gliding Club) on a Sunday afternoon. The wind was too high for hang gliding the day the photograph was taken. 4 April 1976.

Joe Parkins aged 80, and an ex-Sunday School boy of the Methodist Church, The Square, helps to celebrate their 150th anniversary by showing Sunday School children of the church, slides, photographs, and records of the church and town, and explained what life was like when he was a boy at Sunday School. 10 April 1976.

The 'Borough Arms' (Albion Street) football team in the Junior Cup Final at the Town ground, 11 April 1976.

At the saluting base on St George's Day. Left to right: W. Allen (chairman Dunstable & District Scout Council); Richard Markham (chairman, South Beds District Council); Arthur Buck (Scout Commissioner, now retired); Mrs Markham; and the Mayor, Mrs Pat Pocknell. 24 April 1976.

Some of the Cubs who were in the St George's day parade outside the Catholic Church after attending the service, 24 April 1976.

The Mayor, Mrs Pat Pocknell with a party of Belgian Rotarians who visited Dunstable and were entertained by the Rotary Club of Dunstable seen on the Queensway balcony, 30 April 1976.

Arthur Buck (seated with clock) retires as Scout Commissioner. His office was taken over by Bob Taylor (on Arthur's right). Various presentations were made including a garden seat, by Richard Markham, chairman of South Beds District Council. 10 May 1976.

Lancot County Primary school-children 'waiting anxiously' at the school's birthday celebrations, 14 May 1976.

The Mayor Mrs Pocknell 'obliges' by throwing these oranges to them. Enough were thrown to the various classes so that each child received at least one orange (unlike the Dunstable Downs orange rolling see pages 51 and 52). 14 May 1976.

The 1976 carnival and fete organised by the Dunstable Round Table was without doubt the biggest and best carnival ever to be held in Dunstable. Riding in style is the Carnival Queen Sandra Field (on the left) and her two attendants on Whit Monday, 31 May 1976.

The prize-winning float of Cross Paperware, 31 May 1976.

Line-up on the stage, back row: S. J. Molyneaux (Deputy Mayor), Mrs P. Pocknell (Mayor), Ed (Stewpot) Stewart (DJ, radio and television personality), who opened the fete. Mrs and Mr Stewart Clark (Chairman, South Beds District Council) in the front, Janet Davies (attendant to the Queen), Sandra Field (Carnival Queen), and Anita Downing (the other attendant). 31 May 1976.

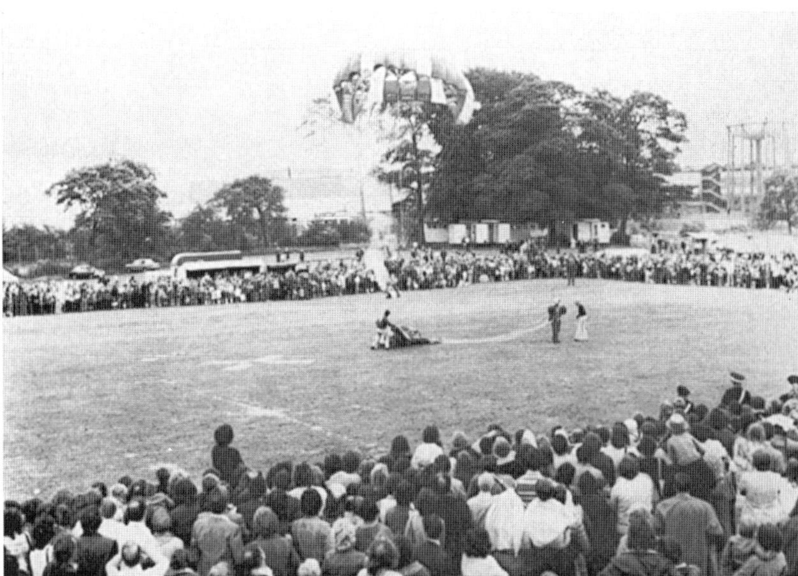

And this was what the 20,000 to 30,000 people who attended were really waiting for – 'The parachute drop' that was late due to bad weather. So ended a great day for Dunstable: let's hope this year proves just as great. 31 May 1976.

Harry Haslam Luton Town manager seen with the trophy winners at the 'Footballer of the year' presentation dinner of AC Delco Football Club, held in their canteen, May 1976.

Manshead School cricket team, 14 July 1976.

The new Health Centre opens (adjacent to Priory Gardens, transferred from Kingsway) and cost £¼ million. Some of the staff seen outside, July 1976.

Model of the proposed new development of the south-west Quadrant, October 1976.

A 'double-hole-in-one': Reg Scott (left) and Reg Higgs, both members of the Dunstable Downs Golf Club, both off a 13 handicap. They achieved what a lot of golfers dream of 'a hole-in-one', but with one difference – they were playing in a competition called the Sanders Fours Trophy. They were both using No 9 irons at the 9th hole, 123 yards. They were not partners. Scott drove first, his ball took one bounce and went in the hole. Higgs drove next (thinking what was the point) and made the identical shot as Scott. A unique achievement you may think but it has now been done 17 times. 9 October 1976.

A few remaining members of the Old Contemptibles stand and watch the Royal British Legion on the occasion of their colours being laid up at a Dedication service held in the Priory Church. The Old Contemptibles were formed after the first world war but with diminishing numbers decided to lay up their colours, and the reformed Dunstable branch of the Royal British Legion did this for them, 10 October 1976.

The band of the Royal Marines visit Northfields School, 22 October 1976.

Some of the children with the drummers. 22 October 1976.

Dunstable Operatic Society Tramps' Supper Dance at the 'Winston Churchill', 22 October 1976.

Ken Woodward, secretary of the Dunstable branch of the National Graphical Association, retires through ill health after ten years. He was presented with an illuminated address and various cheques including one for £600. The new secretary is Steve Bedwell. Picture shows Ken in wheelchair with the new secretary standing behind him, at the United Services Club, 22 October 1976.

Service of Remembrance in Priory Meadow. Extreme left: the Mayor of Dunstable S. J. Molyneaux; fourth from left: S. J. Clark, chairman South Beds District Council, in the centre with medals Robert Cranmer (Chief Executive South Beds District Council) and on his left David Madel, MP, 14 November 1976.

At the Queensway Hall. Terry Hall with 'Lenny the Lion' so well known by many children who watch television.

The last photograph in the book not only ends twenty-five years of Dunstable (1952–77) but also recalls the hottest summer (1976) for many years. These Council gardens were being watered with water from the sewage works. Summer 1976.

Acknowledgements

I offer my personal thanks to the following people whose help has been invaluable
My assistant Kevin Lane
Mr Harold White of White Crescent Press
Mr George Lyle
Miss Carol Ann
Mrs Shirley Mundy
Mr Paul Whiting, Mr Andrew Wallis, and Miss Catherine Seaton of the *Dunstable Gazette*
Mr Michael Kilby
And to all those people who have put up with my endless enquiries.
The Dunstable and Houghton Regis Libraries for letting me use their facilities and the *Dunstable Gazette* for allowing me to use extracts from their papers.

Bruce Turvey

MAYORS OF THE BOROUGH OF DUNSTABLE 1952–74

1949–52 T. Sandland
1952–54 B. J. Scott
1954–56 W. H. Robinson
1956–59 W. T. Lack (awarded OBE in 1960)
1959–61 L. Palmer
1961–62 P. J. Melton
1962–63 Haydn W. Parrott
1963–64 M. L. Kilby (Dunstable's youngest ever Mayor, at the age of 38)
1964–65 L. C. Worby
1965–66 W. Creasey
1966–67 C. W. A. Conway
1967–68 W. Allen
1968–69 P. N. Wainwright
1969–70 R. Wyles
1970–71 L. Mair
1971–73 E. L. Royce
1973–74 W. E. Farbon (the last Mayor of the Borough of Dunstable)

THE CHARTER TRUSTEE MAYORS OF DUNSTABLE

1974-75 E. S. Clark
1975-76 Mrs Pat Pocknell
1976-77 S. J. Molyneaux

TOWN CLERKS OF DUNSTABLE 1952–74

March 1950 to January 1966 Jack Smith
March 1966 to 5 February 1974 Leslie Victor Rallison
7 February to 31 March 1974 Miss Pam Radge (the last Town Clerk of Dunstable)

HONORARY FREEMAN OF THE BOROUGH between 1952 and 1974
Harold William Parrott (a former Mayor 1943–46) in 1959

POPULATION CENSUS 1971 – Dunstable: 31,790

INDEX

Ex-Servicemen's Dinner (Waterlow's), 1958 62

About the Author

Lifelong Dunstablian Bruce Turvey started taking photographs with a box Brownie whilst still a 12 year old at Britain Street (now Priory) school - and by the age of 17½ he had opened a photography business which remained one of the town's best known shops for over 30 years until 1983. He continued however to take bookings from home, until his wedding assignments had totalled almost 4000 by the time he retired a few years ago. and in the 1990s his expertise was still being recognised by no less than four international awards.

Via a press agency in the 1950s some of his pictures appeared in the Fleet Street dailies, and he also later covered many stories for the Dunstable Gazette - who returned the compliment and took the photograph opposite to mark his ruby anniversary in business. Amongst nearly half a million, meticulously - catalogued negatives he treasures the records of countless town events, characters and buildings. The best from his most productive period are captured in this souvenir book.

ADVERTISEMENT FOR THE FIRST EDITION OF THIS BOOK, 1977

25 YEARS OF DUNSTABLE – IN PICTURES

THE BOOK EVERYONE WILL BE TALKING ABOUT—PUBLISHING DATE, CARNIVAL AND FETE DAY JUNE 6th

Bruce Turvey will be pleased to autograph copies of the book, which will be on sale from his stall at the fete on carnival day.

The 400 photographs in this book show the changing face of Dunstable. They show the town as it was and as it is today. There are pictures of landmarks that have gone, like the Town Hall. There are pictures of Church Street before it was widened. There are pictures of some noted Dunstable hotels and public houses that are no longer there.

There are pictures of numerous events, both big and small, from orange rolling on the Downs to dinners, dances and presentations. The sporting life hasn't been forgotten. There are picture including football, rugby, cricket and darts teams.

There are pictures of the many personalities that have visited the town — The Duchess of Gloucester, four Prime Ministers, George Best, Wilfred Pickles, Fred Davis, Raymond Baxter, Bob Monkhouse, David Kossoff, Ed "Stewpot" Stewart.

All the pictures are comprehensively captioned and there is a cross reference index with approximately 700 entries.

You may be among the thousands of faces that are shown in the book. Real "locals" are sure to recognise someone they knew or know.

There is also a written diary by the author, recording interesting pieces of information from the last 25 years. For example, in 1952 detached bungalow, 3 bedrooms, 2 receptions, tiled bathroom, domestic office, detached garage, standing in an acre of land, would have cost you only £3,000. At the same time, a 1950 Rover saloon would have cost you £2,095. In August, 1954, there were only 23 people unemployed in Dunstable.

25 YEARS OF

DUNSTABLE

1952—1977

Commemorating the Silver Jubilee of HM Queen Elizabeth II

A collection of 400 photographs by

BRUCE TURVEY

THE BOOK WILL BE ON GENERAL SALE AFTER THE LAUNCHING DATE, AND AUTOGRAPHED COPIES MAY BE PURCHASED DIRECT FROM THE PUBLISHERS:

TURVEY AND TURVEY (Photographers) LTD
95 High Street North, Dunstable 64354
or obtained from any of the following:

IN DUNSTABLE
ANGLO-CONTINENTAL DELICATESSEN, High St, North
ARMSTRONGS OFF-LICENCE, High Street North
BULL PH, High Street North
CENTRAL CAFE, High Street North
CONSERVATIVE CLUB, High Street North
D.E.A., Albion Street
DORMANS, The Quadrant
DOWNS GARAGE, Tring Road
DUNSTABLE MARKET, Paperback Stall, Queensway park
DUNSTABLE TOWN SUPPORTERS' CLUB, Brewers Hill
D. V. JANE, Newsagent, Albion Street
GOOD FOOD STORE/POST OFFICE, Downside
HIGHWAYMAN PH, London Road
JOHN'S HAIRDRESSERS, High Street North
METHODIST CHURCH, The Square (The Minister)
MOTORFACTORS, Union Street
PAPER KIOSK, see 'Darkie' at the crossroads
PETERSON'S, West Street
PRIORY SERVICE STATION, High Street South
PROFESSIONAL SHOP, DUNSTABLE GOLF CLUB
ST MARY'S CATHOLIC CHURCH (Father Rafferty)
STAR AND GARTER PH, High Street South
STEVE COOK, Church Street
H. TARRY, NEWSAGENT, Chiltern Road
TILLEY'S BUTCHERS, High Street South
THE TRADING POST, High Street South
UNITED SERVICES CLUB, High Street South (the Steward)
VICTORIA CLUB (Alan Potter)
WINSTON CHURCHILL PH, Church Street
OTHER AREAS
HOME COUNTIES COLOUR SERVICES, 12 Leagrave Road, Luton
RED LION, Dagnall
THE VINE, Castle Street, Luton
FACTORIES (for employees only)
ABC TRAVEL GUIDES/INDEX PRINTERS Derek Bird
CROSS PAPERWARE, Ann Dowdswell
WATERLOWS, Personnel Dept.

or where you see the blue and white poster!
Publishing price £4.80.
Trade enquiries welcomed.

A selection of photographs from the book, will be on show in a special '25 years of Dunstable' exhibition which will be held in the Library during the month of June.

The Book Castle
Publishers of Local Interest Titles

HISTORIC INNS OF DUNSTABLE: Vivienne Evans.
Illustrated booklet, especially featuring ten pubs in the town centre.
DUNNO'S ORIGINALS: A facsimile of the rare pre-Victorian history of Dunstable and surrounding villages. New preface and glossary by John Buckledee, Editor of The Dunstable Gazette.
DUNSTAPLELOGIA: Charles Lamborn.
Facsimile of a well-respected mid-Victorian town history, with a number of engravings of local buildings. New introduction by John Buckledee.
DUNSTAPLE: A Tale of the Watling Highway: A.W. Mooring.
Dramatic novelisation of Dunstable's legend of Dunne the Robber - reprinted after a century out of print. New introduction by John Buckledee.
DUNSTABLE SCHOOL: 1888-1971: F.M. Bancroft.
Short history of one of the town's most influential institutions.
DUNSTABLE DOWN THE AGES: Joan Schneider and Vivienne Evans.
Succinct overview of the town's prehistory and history - suitable for all ages.
PROUD HERITAGE: A Brief History of Dunstable, 1000-2000AD:
Vivienne Evans.
Century by century account of the town's rich tradition and key events, many of national significance.
DUNSTABLE WITH THE PRIORY: 1100-1550: Vivienne Evans.
Dramatic growth of Henry I's important new town around a major crossroads.
DUNSTABLE IN TRANSITION: 1550-1700: Vivienne Evans.
Wealth of original material as the town evolves without the Priory.
DUNSTABLE DECADE: THE EIGHTIES: A Collection of Photographs:
Pat Lovering.
A souvenir book of nearly 300 pictures of people and events in the 1980s.
STREETS AHEAD: An Illustrated Guide to the Origins of Dunstable's Street Names: Richard Walden.
Fascinating text and captions to hundreds of photographs, past and present, throughout the town.
DUNSTABLE IN DETAIL: Nigel Benson.
A hundred of the town's buildings and features, plus town trail map.
BOURNE and BRED: A Dunstable Boyhood Between the Wars: Colin Bourne.
An elegantly written, well illustrated book capturing the spirit of the town over fifty years ago.

OLD HOUGHTON: Pat Lovering.
Pictorial record capturing the changing appearances of Houghton Regis over the past 100 years.
ROYAL HOUGHTON: Pat Lovering.
Illustrated history of Houghton Regis from the earliest of times to the present.
A LASTING IMPRESSION: Michael Dundrow.
A boyhood evacuee recalls his years in the Chiltern village of Totternhoe near Dunstable.
STICKS AND STONES: The Life and Times of a Journeyman Printer in Hertford, Dunstable, Cheltenham and Wolverton: Harry Edwards.
Includes Waterlow's in the fifties and sixties.
ELEPHANTS I'LL NEVER FORGET: A Keeper's Life at Whipsnade Zoo: John Weatherhead.
Experiences, dramatic and sad, from a lifetime with these well-loved giants.
WHIPSNADE MY AFRICA: Lucy Pendar.
The inside story of sixty years of this world-renowned institution. Full of history, anecdotes, stories of animals and people.